PENGUIN BOOKS

TALES OF A DALAI LAMA

Pierre Henri Delattre was born in Detroit, Michigan, in 1930, spent his childhood in southern France and received a B.A. from the University of Pennsylvania, an M.A. from the University of Guanajuato, Mexico, and a B.D. from the University of Chicago Divinity School. He has taught at every level from first grade to graduate school, and has contributed articles to *Time*, *Newsweek* and the *New York Times*, and stories and poems to numerous magazines including *Atlantic*, *Playboy* and *Harper's Bazaar*. Pierre Delattre has worked as a cab driver, a railroad switchman and held many industrial jobs over the years, has toured campuses as lecturer on contemporary religious motifs in culture and politics, spent two years as a film maker, directed a television series and ran a coffee house and theatre for five years. During the fifteen years he spent in the San Francisco Bay area, he studied the influence of eastern mysticism on western life styles. Pierre Delattre now lives in Mexico.

D1513709

DRAWINGS BY THE AUTHOR

PIERRE DELATTRE

TALES OF
A DALAI LAMA

PENGUIN BOOKS

Penguin Books Ltd, Harmondsworth, Middlesex, England
Penguin Books, 625 Madison Avenue, New York, New York 10022, U.S.A.
Penguin Books Australia Ltd, Ringwood, Victoria Australia
Penguin Books Canada Ltd, 2801 John Street, Markham, Ontario, Canada L3R 1B4
Penguin Books (N.Z.) Ltd, 182–190 Wairau Road, Auckland 10, New Zealand

—

First published in Great Britain by Victor Gollancz 1972
Published in Penguin Books 1978

—

—

Portions of this book originally appeared in
Harper's Bazaar and *Playboy*

—

Made and printed in Great Britain by
Richard Clay (The Chaucer Press) Ltd,
Bungay, Suffolk
Set in Intertype Lectura

To
John Beauchamp Thompson
who taught me to love
the questions
about
God

Foreword

Few people outside Tibet or India have been fortunate enough to meet the Dalai Lama face to face. Like all charismatic figures, however, he travels far and wide to visit the religious imagination with his mysterious presence. Such is the humor of the holy spirit in search of humanity.

Stated less subtly, and to avoid any possible misunderstanding, let me say clearly and emphatically that this is not a biography but tales of fiction; that the human incarnation even of a Dalai Lama, including the Fourteenth, who is (and may he long remain) among the living, cannot in fact be so very different from other human beings, least of all as a child of tender years; that he appears here not as an individual but in a representative and symbolic capacity; and that in this book fiction is most decidedly stranger than truth.

P. D.

Contents

Contents

Tales of a Dalai Lama

The Dancing Master of Kung Fu

REPORTS reached the Dalai Lama that a certain Master of Kung Fu was roaming the countryside converting young men to the study of violence. Though Tibetan by birth, this man had been raised in Peking and was said to have returned as a secret agent to astonish Tibetans with the superior power of the Chinese in such a way as to render the country open and eager for conquest.

The Master of Kung Fu had made his reputation by taking on eight fierce Lolo warriors who attacked him on a mountain pass, killing seven of them so quickly that the one with the broken legs who survived swore the marvelous voyager had met their attack with movements so swift he seemed merely to walk through them and continue peacefully on his way.

Wherever the Master of Kung Fu stopped, he gathered followers and admirers who were fascinated by the mystical beauty of his methods. The dance of destruction, which he was always glad to perform in slow motion before an audience in the marketplace, was said to be awesomely beautiful. Done swiftly, the dance could not be seen. The master would seem to be standing absolutely still. Only a rush of wind indicated that he had spun about, throwing out his arms and legs in such fashion as to leave at least a dozen of the young toughs who were trying to dodge him grabbing at the parts of their bodies he had playfully flicked with his hands or feet to indicate which bones he could have broken, which organs destroyed.

Against all Buddhist laws, there had been unnecessary slaughter of yaks in order to provide the many husky monks, who had abandoned their lamaseries and robes, with black leather outfits like the one the Master of Kung Fu wore from neck to ankle, his huge muscles making the costume tight as his own flesh.

These leather-sheathed disciples followed their master everywhere challenging each other to duels, many of which ended in death or crippling. The Regent and other advisers to the Dalai Lama were deeply concerned, especially after blasphemous rumors began circulating that the Master of Kung Fu was an incarnation of Shiva, Hindu god of destruction.

There would have been riots had they thrown the man in jail, since he had done nothing wrong. He had a perfect right to be in the country. Not since his brilliant defense against the Lolos had he seriously injured anyone. When government officials questioned his intentions, he said that he was a sincere religious mystic trying to communicate certain cosmic laws learned from his Chinese guru.

It was decided not to attack him publicly but, in conformity with old Tibetan customs when someone claims religious privilege for questionable acts, to invite him most courteously to visit the Dalai Lama.

Pleased with the invitation, the Master of Kung Fu strode into the Dalai Lama's ceremonial hall. Being only ten years old at the time, the young God-King could not help but be impressed with the marvelously potent vibrations he gave off. They reduced the monks and lamas present to womanish giggling and gasping. The Master of Kung Fu was indeed a handsome, dashing fellow with his thick blue-black hair falling down over the shoulders of his leather suit. His teeth flashed confidently under a handlebar mustache. He did not prostrate himself but merely bowed gallantly, then leaned back to fill his chest with air until his whole body seemed to swell, tighten and gleam.

'Your Highness,' he began. 'I know why you asked me here and I want you to stop worrying. Ugliness is my only enemy. You're all beautiful people' – a titter from the monks – 'and I wouldn't think of doing you harm.'

'When you want to do harm,' asked the Dalai Lama, 'what kind of harm can you do?'

'Well, I don't want you to see it as harm at all, Highness. I want you to see it as help. I'm a lover of beauty is what I am, just like any enlightened man. And I know as well as you that you can't raise up beauty in this world without clearing out the ugliness first. You may not be able to see the results right now – in fact it may seem like just the opposite – but what I'm doing is I'm raising up beauty by training a special cadre of men to prepare the ground. That's why I like to do my recruiting from the lamaseries. There's too much ugliness in this world, much too much. Something's got to be done about it by people who can back their strength with moral zeal. I figure the place to start is right here in this country where I was born. I could use your help to get the job done.'

'What exactly do you do?' asked the Dalai Lama.

'Royal Highness, the best way to show you would be for you to stand here in front of me while I do a little dance it took me some fifteen years to perfect. Though I can kill a dozen men instantly with this dance, have no fear. This will only be a demonstration of ugliness destruction. Without seeing these ugly forces destroyed – for my arms and legs move faster than the blades of a helicopter – you will experience the great quietness that comes afterward when they are stilled.'

The Dalai Lama stood up and immediately felt as if a

wind had blown flower petals across his body. He looked down but saw nothing. 'You may proceed,' he told the Master of Kung Fu.

'Proceed?' said the other, grinning jovially. 'I've already finished. What you felt were my hands flicking across your body. If it please Your Highness, this was a demonstration in slow motion, extremely slow motion, of the way I could have destroyed the organs of your body one by one. With this knuckle, I could have severed the contact between your brain and your spine. With the tip of this finger, I could have left you impotent. With the edge of this hand, I could have made it impossible for you to excrete. With this toe, I could have broken your arm while breaking your leg in the same motion with my heel. Your eyes, ears, nose, throat, spleen, liver ... you name it. I could have taken them all out during that one little dance.'

Beaming with pride, he flexed his muscles and looked his body over, up and down, approvingly. 'To achieve the great peace,' he concluded, 'there are demons inside and outside that need to be eradicated. They appear and disappear so rapidly you cannot see them, but I've learned to see them and I can catch them and kill them before they get away, just as you catch a fly.'

'I do not catch flies,' said the Dalai Lama. A murmur of approval went up from the assembled monks. 'No,' said the Dalai Lama, glad to hear that his comrades had not been entirely seduced, 'we do not catch flies in Tibet.'

The Master of Kung Fu seemed momentarily taken aback, but he puffed himself up once more and resumed: 'Quite so. But there is much sickness in this land due to the flies. In China there is very little sickness since every man knows how to catch a fly. Your Highness, I was not brought up in the serene tranquility of this place but in the streets of a city much like your Lhasa only larger. In the city called Peking I looked at eyes muddied from staring through fumes of putrefaction at images of capitalistic lust. I heard mouths speak incessantly to presumed social inferiors in tones full of insult, contempt, dissimulation and vengeance. I have known hearts to beat excitedly over the torture of innocent men. I have watched gluttons with bloated stomachs riding on the backs of starvelings. I have seen legs wobbling pathetically to hold up a body poisoned by chemicals. I have seen ears eagerly bending to rumor, gossip, false reports and greedy evangelisms of all kinds. In short, I have witnessed corruption in every part of man's body and have taken it upon myself to destroy this corruption once and for all.'

'And after it's destroyed?' asked the Dalai Lama.

'It is destroyed. Mine may only be an art of preliminaries but it *is* final. And I am its master.'

'I know a master greater than you,' said the Dalai Lama.

'Without wishing to offend Your Highness, I doubt that very much.'

'Yes, I have a champion who can best you,' insisted the boy king.

'Let him challenge me then, and if he bests me I shall leave Tibet forever.'

'If he bests you, you shall have no need to leave Tibet.' The Dalai Lama looked around to see if his monks were as confident as he was, but they all looked very disconsolate. The huge guards were looking away, hoping he wouldn't call on one of them; and the others were looking at the guards, obviously convinced that not one of them stood the slightest chance.

The Dalai Lama clapped his hands. 'Regent,' he said, 'summon the Dancing Master, and while we're waiting let's have some tea.'

The tea ceremony was just about over when the Regent

returned with the Dancing Master. He was a wiry little fellow, half the size of the Master of Kung Fu and well past his prime. His legs were entwined with varicose veins and he was swollen at the elbows from arthritis. Nevertheless, his eyes were glittering merrily and he seemed eager for the challenge.

The Master of Kung Fu did not mock his opponent. 'My own guru,' he said, 'was even smaller and older than you, yet I was unable to best him until last year. I could have finished him easily had I ever been able to touch him, but he moved too fast. Only last year did I finally catch him on the ear and destroy him, as I shall destroy you when you finally tire. To show that I know your methods and won't be tricked into exhausting my energy, I shall first let you strike me at will. Your frail little hands can do me no harm while I'm at full strength.'

The two opponents faced off. The Master of Kung Fu was taking a jaunty, indifferent stance, tempting the other to attack.

The old Dancing Master began to swirl very slowly, his robes wafting around his head. His arms stretched out and his hands fluttered like butterflies toward the eyes of his opponent. The fingers settled gently for a moment upon the bushy eyebrows. The Master of Kung Fu drew back in astonishment. He looked around the great hall. Everything was suddenly vibrant with rich hues of singing color. The faces of the monks were radiantly beautiful. It was as if his eyes had been washed clean for the first time.

The fingers of the Dancing Master stroked the nose of the Master of Kung Fu and suddenly he could smell pungent barley from a granary in the city far below. He could smell butter melting in the most fragrant of teas, as the Dalai Lama, incomparably beautiful, sipped tea and watched him calmly. A flicking of the Dancing Master's foot at his genitals, and his penis was throbbing with desire, pushing to break loose from its leather-bound sheath. The sound of a woman singing through an open window filled him with exquisite yearning to draw her into his arms and caress her. He found himself removing his leather clothes until he stood naked before the Dancing Master, who was now assaulting him with joy at every touch.

His body began to hum like a finely tuned instrument. He could hear the great horns resounding in a thousand rooms of the Potala, praising creation. He opened his mouth and sang like a bird at sunrise. It seemed to him that he was possessed of many arms, legs and hands, and all wanted to nurture the blossoming of life.

The Master of Kung Fu began the most beautiful dance that had ever been seen in the great ceremonial hall of the Grand Potala. It lasted for three days and nights, during which time everyone in Tibet feasted and visitors crowded the doorways and galleries to watch.

Only when he finally collapsed at the throne of the Dalai Lama did he realize that another body was lying beside him. The old Dancing Master had died of exertion while performing his final and most marvelous dance. But he had died happily, having found the disciple he had always yearned for. The new Dancing Master of Tibet took the frail corpse in his arms and, weeping with love, drew the last of its energy into his body. Never had he felt so strong.

The Compassion of the Elephant

Two elephants lived in the Jewelled Garden, gifts to the Dalai Lama from the Maharajah of Jaipur. The elephants were very much in love and spent their time walking side by side along the paths, careful not to tread on the flowers. The Dalai Lama would often sit on a bench watching them. He especially liked to watch them copulate.

It took the male elephant seven days to stimulate his mate, three days to dig the pit with his tusks in which she would stand, a day to enter her and two weeks to copulate. The orgasm lasted forty-seven hours, during which the shrieks of the cow and the groans of the bull shook the walls of the Potala and could be heard even in the streets of Lhasa, where everyone remained very still to listen.

The Dalai Lama had gone into the garden one afternoon for meditation. The cow was in her pit and the bull was just entering her. His thrusts in and out were so long and deep and slow that each one lasted as long as it takes a satellite to orbit the earth.

He decided not to leave the garden until the copulation was over. When the orgasm was only a day away, he instructed his servants to bring him no more food or drink and to leave him uninterrupted so that he might be truly at one with his beasts. Breathing slowly through one nostril at a time, holding for long periods before exhalation, the Dalai Lama slowly put himself into a trance.

As the orgasm approached, he began to feel all elements in the cosmos rushing together. Lovers were running into each other's arms. Tradesmen were hurrying to the market-places. Bees were gathering to their hives. Even the stars were streaking toward collision. Rivers in his own arms were rushing toward the sea, as his body amassed itself into a single muscle.

The explosion came.

There was a flash of blinding white light in the mind of the Dalai Lama. Once more he was creating the world. With tremendous roars and groans and screams, milk pouring from his breasts, tears from his eyes, he gave off the world. It spread out before him, stars and sands, rocks and living things fanning out from the center into infinite space. When he had created farther than his mind could reach, he breathed it all in again, drew it together into the clutch of his heart and sent it out once more. Worlds were born and died, and the elephants finally lay down on their sides and slept.

The Dalai Lama was being shaken. 'Wake up, Your Highness,' said the Regent, lifting the boy up in his powerful arms. 'You must come in from the cold. You must drink and eat. Your body's almost burned out.'

They fed the Dalai Lama and tucked him into bed. He always slept most soundly after the elephants.

The meditation on elephants ended in a most tragic way. As a good-will gesture, the Russians sent the Dalai Lama a small caterpillar tractor to facilitate plowing in the vegetable section of his garden, which was quite large. Fascinated by the yellow machine, the elephants would follow it up and down the furrows, much to the annoyance of the Russian technician, who dared not complain. Finally, the technician lost patience and, to scare the elephants away, suddenly backed the tractor toward them. The cow

did not step back in time and her foot was run over at its edge.

She let out a shriek that brought the Dalai Lama rushing from his prayers, too late to save the Russian, who had been seized in the bull's trunk and smashed repeatedly against the wall. What ensued was like a hurricane. While the female spun frantically on three feet, the male went into a panic, running in circles through the garden trampling flowers, knocking down bushes and uprooting trees until every plant had been destroyed. By this time, the cow had lain down on her side. The bull tried to console her with grunts and nudges. She was quiet now but his wailing increased. He could not bear her pain.

The Dalai Lama ordered his guards into the garden to help the elephant, but her mate attacked them ferociously until there was nothing to do but stand on the roofs and balconies watching the agony.

It was not so much the agony of the wounded cow that impressed the Dalai Lama as the agony of her mate, who never ceased to wail and moan during the two weeks it took her to die. A day later, the bull was dead, too, of sorrow. Within this sorrow was stored such an enormous energy of love that the monks were instructed to form a circle on the roofs around the garden and to hold hands.

They stood in their robes like a garland of red and yellow flowers, waiting for that powerful radiance of love to come out into them. The Dalai Lama was with them in the circle. He held the hands of two ancient lamas, and when the male elephant finally rolled down beside his mate and expired, the God-King joined with the others in drawing that energy up into the circle – the slow, giant compassion of the elephant. It was night and their circle glowed with an orange light. They were like the rim of a huge butter lamp with the flame at their center blown out, but the light still captured and glowing in the butter.

The wilting flowers and the dying trees were lit up for an instant, then all was dark. The monks returned to their chapels and the Dalai Lama, aglow with love, returned to his room.

Mrs Tibet

EVERY year a beauty contest was held in Tibet and a Mrs Tibet was chosen by popular vote.

It must be understood, however, that female beauty in Tibet is judged by how successfully a woman protects the spiritual privacy of her husband; therefore, the winner of the beauty contest invariably appears to be extremely ugly.

Everyone knows better, of course. They know from the merriness of her husband when he occasionally goes out for a stroll that his wife's ugliness is only a sham and that, once sequestered with him behind the walls, she becomes transformed into the loveliest of women. But they also appreciate that her beauty comes from complete devotion to the spiritual peace of his household. This requires that she act in public like a snarling dog who only lets visitors with exceptionally peaceful and loving vibrations pass through the door – and these only when her husband is resting from creative work and meditation and does not mind the interruption.

These most beautiful women are called gargoyles and are much venerated for their ability to make saints of their men by spending so much time on the doorstep of the house looking vicious, surly, shrewish and generally unpleasant. The very sight of them makes a person cross the street, or even turn around and go the other way, due to a foul odor they sometimes give off.

It is believed that many a man of spiritual depth was

brought to a higher level of consciousness and the promise of an exalted reincarnation by his protective gargoyle. The reward for such women – so this rather male-oriented civilization believes – is to become reincarnated as men blessed with wives of seemingly frightful ugliness.

The Dalai Lama was only three years old and had just assumed the throne when he was asked to crown Mrs Tibet of 1940. Screaming, spitting and cursing, she was dragged in before him and shoved down on her knees to receive the crown. Three strong monks had to restrain her. A gag was stuffed into her mouth to shut her up long enough to allow the terrified baby king to place the crown hastily on her head.

The moment she was crowned, however, his divine presence was privileged to see for a short while that exquisite loveliness otherwise reserved only for her husband. A halo appeared above her head. She became so soft that the hands restraining her fell away. She stood up gracefully and curtsied all around, while the ten thousand monks who had been watching suddenly were hushed. The lines of her face vanished and her mouth turned up in a voluptuous smile that made her eyes shine with merciful heavenly beauty.

As if she were his own mother, she did not hesitate to ascend the throne and sit down next to the little Dalai Lama. Happily, he let her take his head to her swelling breasts. She stroked his hair until he fell sound asleep.

He was awakened by the Regent to find himself in his own bedroom, propped up on pillows and smelling of milk and mother's hair. Mrs Tibet, he was told, had turned ugly again, as was her custom, and not wishing to shock her king, had carried him to his bed, covered him up tenderly and returned to the portal of her husband's house, where even now she was sitting in the dust snarling.

A Plastic Watering Can

THE Dalai Lama's emissary to Washington was asked how the Dalai Lama viewed American foreign aid. He replied, 'My king sees a plastic watering can in the garden of the world.' Few reporters would be able to interpret this without the help of the following story.

The Dalai Lama entered the Jewelled Garden one spring with a plastic watering can given to him by the wife of the American ambassador to India. The can was green with a yellow spout.

After watering all the flowers, he left the watering can in a corner of the garden.

The next day he discovered that all the flowers had wilted.

He consulted a horticulturalist, who could not explain how this had come to pass.

He consulted a physicist, who was just as baffled.

He consulted an artist and received the right answer immediately: 'There's a dead color at the corner of your canvas. Remove it and the colors will come alive again.'

The Dalai Lama removed the watering can and, presto! The petals filled with syrup, while green juice shot up into the stems and leaves until the flowers once more were reaching for the sun.

Kites

DURING his early years as king, the Dalai Lama loved nothing better than to stand on the roof of the Potala and watch the kites flying. He was not allowed to fly a kite of his own. As the Regent had put it: 'You cannot have a kite because you already *are* a kite. Having is compensation for not being. Since you can be all things, you need have nothing.' Years later, the Dalai Lama's friend Dr Klune, an itinerant holy man, further clarified this by saying, 'Whatever you cannot have, dear King, you must be. If you cannot have a bicycle, be a bicycle. If you cannot have a girl friend, be a girl friend. If you cannot have a work of art, be a work of art. Be a chair, be a book, be a kite. Be a Dalai Lama.'

The winning kite in the kite festivals was regarded as the symbolic image of the king's heavenly presence. All day long he would watch the kites to see which would be the last one left in the sky, for the last one was himself and every kite that fell from around him made him feel at once more triumphant and more lonely. He was like a man who watches himself rise in spiritual consciousness, leaving more and more friends behind with each new cosmic breath until he finds himself high up and quite alone.

The game took place behind a row of trees so that the Dalai Lama could only see the kites and not the people who flew them, though he could hear the high-pitched shouting of the children as they struggled to possess the vanquished kites that fell. Each kite was attached to a ball of string covered with a kind of glue made with powdered glass. The game was to fly one's kite in such a way that one's string cut the string of someone else's kite, causing it to wobble crazily and then go twisting down to earth. The Dalai Lama could watch the multicolored kites swerving back and forth, dodging and pursuing each other until only one was left in the sky – and that kite, so his mentors told him time and again with delight, was his own sweet spirit fluttering above his people.

One sunny afternoon, the little Dalai Lama was riding in his sedan chair on the shoulders of his subjects looking out through his golden curtain at the sky when he thought: I'm going to become a kite. Right now I'm going to spread my arms and fly. He stepped out from his sanctuary and stood in full view of his people, his legs spread wide and his arms outstretched, so that his maroon and saffron robe crackled like tight paper in the wind.

The procession stopped. The people fell on their faces, not daring to look up. The Dalai Lama saw himself flying into the sky. He was fluttering around up there high above the crowd, exhilarated, walking on air. He swooped, he glided, he hovered over them.

'Look up, O my people,' he cried. 'Stand and lift your faces.'

In unison the people arose. He was alone up there, the last kite in the sky, Lord Cutter of All Strings. The Liberator!

But now he saw in the distance another huge kite moving toward him, its enormous silver cord lashing dangerously through the air with sounds like a gale whipping through high rocky mountain passes. Its string was flashing in the sunlight, mixing up tornadoes, as it moved closer and closer to his own frail string, which it finally struck out at and snipped with a mighty *whoosh*.

Uttering the cry of a newborn babe, he fell to earth. The children scrambled to possess him, screaming and clawing until a mother rushed amongst them, as if to save her own infant from the fangs of wolves. She drew him to her breast and hurried away, hiding him under her shawl. He began to suckle frantically.

The Dalai Lama, six years old, woke up in his bed in the arms of the old Regent. He touched his aching forehead and felt a large welt.

'You fell from your chair, Lord,' said the Regent.

'Wasn't I flying?'

'You were falling, Lord. You bumped your head.'

'Did I make a fool of myself?'

'Whatever you made of yourself, we have made a teaching of God.' And it was so, since a pagoda is erected anywhere in Tibet that the Dalai Lama lies down.

Many devout people came to worship at that spot and one of the great lamas had a vision there of the Buddha of Mercy.

Yet the Dalai Lama never could get used to the idea that a kite would fall instead of rising after its string was cut. Though he saw the strings cut time and again, though he was continually observing the fall of kites from the sky, he was astounded every time they fell. He felt sure that if he ever truly became a kite he would rise until he had disappeared from the eyes of all people once and for all. He could not be turned away forever in his flight to the sun, forever reincarnated into another round of ceremonies and intrigues at the palace.

When he searched into the memory beyond his current incarnation, he could remember many times when the great kite had come flapping toward him with furious sound. He had welcomed it, believing this time that when the cord was cut he would surely rise. He would surely not cry out again

and be born. But, each time, he would awaken to find himself spinning awkwardly downward, until the woman came to snatch him from the devourers and hide him safely to her breast.

Finally the truth was told to him by a court magician: that the kite can only soar because of its tension with the ground. Without the man on the ground, there can be no man in the air, any more than there can be a God-King without a people of faith. No heaven without earth, no god without man, no transcendence without immanence.

The magician brought in a short-wave radio and together he and the boy listened to its hum. 'A piece of cheap machinery,' said the magician, 'metals, wires, glass. Yet we can hear the great Hum in its belly.'

The little boy God thought that he understood, but it wasn't until years later, when he was in exile and curious tourists with cameras were breaking into his privacy to have a skeptical look at this so-called deity, that he began to understand truly how marvelous it was that he, a mere toy of his people, could take such flight when they held the string wrapped around their faithful wrists.

The Oceanic Mind

EVERY evening for an hour the Dalai Lama would stand on his head on a mat in the corner of his room so that the rivers would flow down to the sea.

He could feel the oceanic mind most alive at this hour with thoughts moving like great schools of fish, and fresh illuminations flitting among the reefs.

The Dada Dalai Lama

ALL Englishmen the Dalai Lama had ever met spoke with a stammer when they were most sincere. Looking for the quintessence of what they wished to say, their lips and tongue would *putt-putt* toward it, stall around the edges and finally crash into it with an expression of sour misgiving.

A British visiting poet, for example, upon being asked to suggest one modern poem exemplary of the spirit of his land, seemed on the very rack trying to stammer out the title. His lips and tongue changed course several times. Once, while the first consonant was still only a series of fragile implosions from the pursed lips, the poet blushed profusely and suddenly changed the shape of his mouth altogether into that of a grunting pig.

The Dalai Lama realized that the Englishman had been tempted to suggest a poem of his own but had backed away from fear of being seen naked. Now, at last, the first word of someone else's masterpiece was on its way out. 'R-r-r-r ... R-r-r-r-r ... R-r-r-r-r rage ... Let me see. Yes, I'd say quite the best and most exem-m m-pry contem-m m-pry pem I can think of, Your H-h-h-highness, though mind you it doesn't necessarily represent Her Majesty's dominion as a whole ... T-t-t-thomas, you understand, was in no conceivable sense at all the pet laureate, or even you might say one of the er-r-r ... establishment. No, he was one of those d-d-desperate breed of outriders, yet curiously

35

English, though Welsh, curiously representative and certainly influential more than anyone else since, let us say, El-Eliot to influence ... but to get to the point, Your Highness, the pem I have in mind goes like this, and I think it will show you how the English spirit will never die, indeed, refuses to die. Let me see.'

At this point, the British poet pushed his hand into his vest, assumed a stance with one leg forward and, pointing to the right, threw his gnarled hair back, cleared his throat, adjusted the allure of his eyes, reflected for a moment, nodded, smiled, said, 'Yes,' and attempted seriously to begin. The tongue, however, came up hard on the backside of the gums, its tip pressed so hard there that the word got stuck for some time before extricating itself rudely into a 'D! ... Do! ... Do not go gentle into that good night.'

Long after the poet had presented his cordial invitation to England on behalf of the royal family, the Dada Dalai Lama (as the poet called him) stood musing over the incomprehensible conclusion of the poem recited to him: *Rage, rage against the dying of the light.* Surely the poem had something to do with passing of the soul into another body, but what was this reference to the dying of the light? The dying of what light? Certainly there was no dying of the light after death when one became part of a cosmic brilliance so intense that, even on short teleportations during meditation at night, the Dalai Lama would return to his body feeling that he had been staring too long at the sun.

This Dylan Thomas had certainly worked himself into a rage over nothing. Unless, of course, the rage ... yes, that was it. In his fatuous rage against his father's death, Dylan Thomas had cast a shadow across the source of light within himself. And perhaps the English stammer, like the final language of a dying Christian empire, could be heard as the sputtering of a flame hungry for new spiritual food.

Erase and Record Again

THE Dalai Lama took the portable tape recorder he had received as a gift from the Japanese legation up to the roof of the Potala on a very still night. He pressed the *record* button and went to sleep. Awakened by the sound of the tape's tail flapping, he ran the tape back and listened very attentively. He could hear the galaxy droning slowly around and around through space.

He could remember how he had created the cosmos. He ran the tape back and recorded his words:

> Let there be those, let there be these.
> Let there be fish, let there be trees.
> Let there be fowl, let there be fair.
> Let there be here, let there be there.
> Let there be water, let there be air.
> Let there be fire, let there be earth.
> Let there be death, let there be birth.
> Let there be good, let there be evil.
> Let there be grass, let there be blue.
> Let there be me, let there be you . . .

On and on went his voice into the microphone, naming everything he could think of until the tape ran out. He erased it and started over. He erased the cave men and the dinosaurs, he erased the prayer councils and the wars, he erased rain dances, shaman trances, erased scimitars and lances. He just kept erasing the old and replacing it with new, and the words revolved endlessly on the wheel in easy poetry, born and dying in his mind like so many uncountable stars blazing and burning out.

When he was tired, he slept again while the voices overhead in the celestial dome hummed on.

The Dalai Lama of Flowers

I was told by an eminent botanist that high up the slope of Minya Konkka, shooting through the snow, grew a remarkable primrose, called *Primula glacialis*, one of the very rarest flowers in the world ... It rivalled the sky in the purity of its colour and delicacy of its contours. After I had travelled so much in some of the highest mountains in Asia, I became baffled by the hidden mystery of flowers. Why did the most beautiful, most enchanting and delicate blossoms on the planet grow so high and under such impossibly hard conditions, braving frost, hail, landslides and cruel winds, out of reach of humanity? Were they there by an accident of creation or were they there to please with their unsurpassed beauty eyes other than those of men? Surely man had no business to be where they grew, in places mostly inaccessible to him. Did the *Primula glacialis* perhaps display its sublime flowers for a divinity whose spirit alone brooded in such lofty desolation?

– Peter Goullart

DEAR MR GOULLART:

The relation of height to spirituality is not merely metaphorical. It is a physical reality. The most spiritual people on this planet live in the highest places. So do the most spiritual flowers. But all of life, high and low, is imbued with God and *is* God. I am God and I should know. Like vapor from the earth, all creation ascends and descends; but since the creation is round, this movement appears as contraction and expansion – the breath: OM.

40

I call the high and light aspect of my being *spirit* and the dark and heavy aspect *soul*.

Soul is at home in the deep, shaded valleys. Heavy, torpid flowers saturated with black grow there. The rivers flow like warm syrup. They empty into huge oceans of soul.

Spirit is a land of high, white peaks and glittering jewel-like lakes and flowers. Life is sparse and sounds travel great distances.

There is soul music, soul food, soul dancing and soul love; and there is the same of spirit.

My people were conceived when my soul in the form of a monkey went up from the jungle to ravish the demoness who lived among the snowy peaks. In me, spirit and soul were united as the herdsmen of the high plateaus. When the soul triumphed, the herdsmen came to the lamaseries, for soul is communal and loves humming in unison. But the creative craves spirit. Out of the jungle of the lamasery, the most beautiful monks one day bid farewell to their comrades and go to make their solitary journey toward the peaks, there to mate with the cosmos. What they leave behind, like a pure drop of their passion for God, is the *Primula glacialis*, Dalai Lama of the flowers.

Mr Goullart, no spirit broods over lofty desolation; for desolation is of the depths, as is brooding. At these heights, spirit leaves soul far behind. To the *Primula glacialis*, wind, landslides, hail and frost are not 'cruel,' for all these elements are as high as the flower. Perhaps someday, you will learn that your people need to climb the mountain not simply 'because it is there,' but because the soulful divinity needs to be mated with spirit. May you have the pleasure someday as I did of seeing her from above, like a flower trembling in the wind with all her fragile petals spread; and may you descend upon her gently like the snow.

Sincerely,
THE FOURTEENTH DALAI LAMA OF TIBET

Seven Puffs on a Cigarette

THE Dalai Lama did a few sneaky things in his time just to ease the pressure of having to be so good. Once he even smoked a cigarette, a sin strictly prohibited in Tibet. He was five years old at the time. He had received a confidential package from an advertising agency in the United States of America. Enclosed was a package of Camel cigarettes with a picture of the camel on the front. The Dalai Lama was intrigued by camels because it was said that they could store enough water in their humps to last them for weeks. One of his previous incarnations – the seventh – had been able to do the same thing, storing the water in his mind.

Though he knew that it was wrong, the Dalai Lama was sorely tempted to smoke just one cigarette and throw the others away, if only to understand camels better. A letter enclosed with the package broke down his final resistance. The letter was from Kentucky Agency and read:

YOUR DIVINE AND ROYAL HIGHNESS:

As you may know, prosperity in the United States has been threatened by a breakdown in the Southern way of life. Our people are losing interest in regional products and are searching for more exotic stimulation. Zen Buddhism, Japanese Haiku, Turkish water pipes ... The list grows endless. We would never try to destroy your way of life by bringing our products into your country. We at Kentucky Agency vow to do our sacred utmost to promote your sovereignty and well-being against foreign intrusion. In exchange, we wonder if you would do us a favor. Support our independence by smoking a few of our cigarettes. If you like them, write us a small note of endorsement. The tobacco industry would be eternally grateful if it could tell the people of this land that the famous Dalai Lama smokes Camels. Just sign the testimonial and return it to us via the enclosed self-addressed envelope. A check for fifty thousand dollars to encourage your own local industries will follow on receipt of same.

> With humble gratitude,
> STARR LEE BEAUCHAMP III
> President

The Dalai Lama took one Camel from the package and went up on the balcony to smoke. He lit up and inhaled all the daylight. Darkness ensued. He became a camel holding his breath and looking at the desert stars in wonder, while an Arab sheik sat astride him cooled by the waters in the humps. Finally, he gave out a long sigh and from his muzzle came the morning. The morning brightened into midday and midday burned across the sand dunes through afternoon. A light tap from the sheik's stick and he began to breathe the light back in until it was night again. Seven times the Dalai Lama puffed on the cigarette and seven times the world chaos took form, held its breath and dissolved, while the camel stood there in the desert with the dreaming sheik on its back.

Afterward, the Dalai Lama filled in the testimonial with these words: 'I cannot publicly endorse your camels, but I want you privately to know that each one contains a world of smoking.'

'Everyone Loves the Beautiful
Death of Soldiers'
– Song of a Tibetan camp follower

THE following short speech was delivered to the Tibetan Army by the nine-year-old Dalai Lama at the funeral of a young soldier killed during a border skirmish with the Chinese:

Every warrior goes into battle with a vision of peace.

Every man of peace goes to the temple to watch the gods war with the devils.

The most beautiful spirits ever to enter the heavens are the spirits of soldiers rising from the battlefields.

We are terrified by soldiers when they live, but when they die we love the peace that settles on their faces.

My brave and troubled soldiers, do not expect us to love you while you live, but take consolation in knowing that we love your deaths far more than the deaths of priests whose pent-up rage breaks out upon their flesh when the spirit departs, turning their faces into hideous masks.

Celestial Sports

'I DON'T understand,' said the Dalai Lama. 'Why should anyone be playing against anyone else? Everyone tries to keep the ball in the air. That's all there is to it. When the ball hits the ground, it's a sad moment for everyone and you'll notice how they take a moment to console the person responsible.'

He and the Swedish professor of philosophy were watching a game of ball, and the professor was confused since nobody seemed to be playing against anyone else. Everybody wore the same color uniform as the ball was batted back and forth over a net. 'In our country,' he tried to explain to the king, 'we divide into opposing sides and then we try to make the others miss the ball.'

The Dalai Lama found this quite distressing. 'But then the ball must hit the ground all the time!'

'Your Highness! Why are you weeping?'

'Such a way to play with the human spirit,' sobbed the boy. Deeply shaken, he went to his room to pray.

Seated alone on the roof of the Potala, watching the game through field glasses, the Swedish professor was transported back to his classroom. He saw the students batting an idea across the aisle between the chairs and the podium. He saw himself ruthlessly knocking it to the ground. He saw himself launching a philosophical concept. He saw his students doing their best to oppose it, while they passed contemptuous glances and bided their

47

time until the flaw in his scholarship would be exposed and his position overthrown. The professor longed for a change in the rules so that all together they might keep ideas in the air until the human spirit could take flight. He realized how the Dalai Lama's sadness over the game was only a reflection of the king's disappointment with him, for he had never ceased picking away at Tibetan religious concepts during their interview, detecting the flaw each time and batting the idea right down before it had a chance to survive. Ashamed, he left the palace with but one desire: to get back to Sweden and change the rules of the game.

Meanwhile, the Dalai Lama had become so discouraged about the practice of athletics in other parts of the world that he had second thoughts about allowing his Austrian friend, Harrer, to build a tennis court in the field below the Potala. He was so grateful for the movie camera Harrer had given him, however, that he finally acceded to the request, but with the stipulation that a wall be built high enough so that he would not be tempted to watch the game from his roof.

When curiosity did get the better of him and he looked down through his telescope, all he could see was the judge who sat just above the line of vision in a green tower watching the hidden game. The judge must have felt as grieved as the Dalai Lama over crude European notions of sports as competition because he was forever shaking his head from side to side in despair.

One could ask whether Tibetans are not just as fiercely competitive when they try to cut the strings of each other's kites. Not so. The game played with kite strings rubbed with ground glass symbolizes the cutting of the cord that keeps a child bound to his mother and the human spirit bound to the earth. Though kites fall when the string is

cut, the spirit soars ever upward. Little boys fight over the bodies of those who fall, just as vultures fight over chunks of human flesh after the soul has departed. There is no greater honor in Tibet than to have one's dead body eaten by vultures or to have one's fallen kite torn apart by little boys at play. The aim of the game, as of all life, is to assist in one another's release to higher levels of consciousness. The kite flying is a game that cheers the Dalai Lama's heart when the laughter it evokes rises to the roof of the Potala. There is no cursing or muttering of false congratulation, as so often can be heard exploding from behind the walls of the tennis court.

The vibrations emanating from the tennis court became so bad that the Dalai Lama sent a respected lama out to observe. The lama reported that when Harrer's opponent, an Irish hydraulic engineer named O'Gore, who had just created a dam for them on the Fiery Tooth River, lost a set he would invariably throw his racket into the air and go into a strange dance – a stamping of his feet, shaking of his fists and whirling about while crouched over.

One afternoon, O'Gore went into his dance more enthusiastically than ever before. He had just lost the finals of the Lhasa Foreign Advisers' Lawn Tennis Association Championships. When the dance was over, it began to rain. Suddenly, the observing lama understood. This O'Gore obviously knew how to control water and this must be nothing less than the sacred Irish rain dance.

The Dalai Lama's new movie camera was brought in to absorb the dance the very next time it occurred. The chief sorcerer studied the developed film until he had learned to imitate the dance to perfection. He found that it could bring down the rain without fail.

A Confucian Reprimand

My dear King,

Recently, while in flight from my own country, I had occasion to take refuge in yours. I wish first to thank you for your hospitality. As a rather meticulous Confucian, I'm sure that I made quite a humorous impression upon you; and yet I felt that you came to respect me. When I left, you asked me to tell you frankly what I thought could be done to improve your country and to strengthen it against the inevitable day when China attempts to subject you to her materialistic designs. Out of politeness, I said nothing. In truth, however, I was deeply troubled about my visit to your palace and its lamasery. I have decided that I could best honor you with a few helpful criticisms.

Venerable Sir, you must stop leaving your room in such a mess. The same goes for your lamas and monks, whose living quarters and places of prayer are a scandal to that gracious order which you have such an opportunity to exemplify.

Your Potala is a holy hive. Every room needs to hum and breathe with clean, fresh air. You cannot simply abandon room after room as it fills up with broken pots, beads, bells, torn *tankas* and all the other discarded accoutrements of meditative life. *There is no such thing as slovenly bliss.* What kind of a God do you think you are to allow guests to pass through that pigsty of a royal kitchen into air polluted with the dirt of smoking lamps?

The people look to you. When social endeavor is truly good it is ordered to the cosmic harmony. Every movement, like music, must hum just so. Divine order begins with rising promptly, Your Highness, as soon as the first bell tolls. It continues with the cold bath, the prayer, the greeting of the sun, the breathing, the standing on head and other yoga exercises, dressing with careful attention to every fold of one's robe, putting one's room in order so that each object on floor or wall or table achieves its vibration by a beautiful and useful relation to every other. It gains momentum and purpose as one leaves one's room with properly measured steps, correct posture and purposeful direction.

Such behavior, dear King, cannot be reserved for the infrequent ceremonials but must be observed at all times, in private as well as before men and gods. Otherwise, how can you expect anything different from your subjects — and look at them! Go out into the villages and have a good look at their homes if, indeed, you can find them, for many are literally buried to the roof in cast-off filth. When the Communist invaders come with their clean-up campaigns and their sanitation drives, you must bear responsibility.

You are nearing your thirteenth birthday. As a humble favor to me, I would ask that you begin by straightening your closet, arranging your drapes, cleaning the Buddha on your dresser and neatly ordering the sacred objects in the drawers. Pick up the several slippers thrown in a corner and place them in a neat row under your tea table. Send your soiled clothing to the laundry, wash yourself with a good scented soap, scrub your teeth, brush your hair, put on a clean, well-ironed robe, be prompt in visiting each of your tutors, eat slowly and don't speak with food in your mouth, drink your tea without making noises and see, Holiness, if it doesn't make you feel a little bit more like the God that you are. Gods, too, can lose their identity through sloth.

Attend to the trivia of your life and everything that follows shall be made great.

With hope that these words will be received in the same loving spirit that prompted them,

Very truly yours,

H. CHEN, ESQ.
Faculty Oriental Studies
Oxford University
England

The Soul Collection

EVERY boy has a hobby. The Dalai Lama was no exception. Since he was only allowed to concern himself with spiritual matters, he collected soul impressions and kept them in a large album.

Generally, people regarded their souls in one of five ways: (1) above the head like a halo; (2) in the breast like a vague yearning; (3) enveloping the body like a shroud; (4) moving up and down the spine like an electrical charge; (5) in the pit of the stomach.

There were exceptions which the Dalai Lama kept under a separate category as Freak Souls: Souls in the palms of the hands; souls between the eyes; souls like wings on the back; souls departed from the body on a journey of their own; etc.

Some few cards were returned with the notation, 'No soul,' or 'I have no soul that I know of.' These the Dalai Lama listed in a section called The Innocents.

For each soul, the Dalai Lama also did a drawing in his *Cosmic Coloring Book*. He drew his own soul as a kite. Here are a few of the soul impressions that inspired the most beautiful drawings:

My soul is the cottage by a river waiting for me.

— *Henri Jaccard*

My soul is like the inside of a flame.

— *Halifa Habibi*

54

I am still pursuing my soul with a spear.
>   — *Mr Curly of New Guinea*

My soul is the image I have of myself as I most perfectly wish myself to be: an old man, very lean, very clear-eyed with an expression of bemused sadness that recognizes life as a tragedy yet finds it amusing and good. My soul is free, homeless, owns nothing and is owned by nobody. All he carries with him is a bedroll, a flute, a notebook and a pen. Though extremely kind, my soul is prepared to defend himself. He is a jack-of-all-trades, a musician and a storyteller. When he has traveled many miles he will lie down alone in a high valley and go to sleep.

>   — *Alan Dienstag*

Immutable Light

>   — *Richard Roberts*

I've kissed my soul off to the cosmos.
>   — *Daveed di Barabar*

These soul impressions are still being collected through personal contacts and correspondence with people great and small throughout the world. Many are in answer to a simple form letter that says:

DEAR SIR OR MADAME OR MISS
It would please me very much if you could take time out from your busy life to answer the following question on the line below and return the self-addressed card to me. The question is this: *How do you see your soul?*

The album with the thousands of answers and the coloring book that accompanies it will be collectors' items if ever released by the Dalai Lama from his refuge in India. Those who have answered the card may not realize with whom they are corresponding, since the receiving address is a post-office box in Burma and the signature is simply AN INTERESTED BOY.

The Sire of a Nation

In 1950, when the Chinese invaded Tibet, the Dalai Lama attempted to flee. His people wouldn't let him go. They made no effort to restrain him, but wherever his caravan passed there was such an atmosphere of mourning, such darkness descending on the land, that he could bear it no longer.

Nearing the border, he ordered his caravan to turn around and head back for Lhasa. He knew now that he was truly their father. They never would be able to cope with life outside the lamaistic home he had raised them in. He was the All-Radiant One, Holy of Holies, Source of Light and Wisdom, Jewel in the Lotus, the Ocean.

It was he, Chenrezi, disguised as a monkey, who had seduced the mother of Tibet. He, the Dalai Lama, was the same who had planted the first Tibetan in the womb of the demoness. He may have looked like a boy, but to his people he was the great bull ape. This ungrown virgin was nevertheless the one who could peek out through the golden curtains of his palanquin upon the hordes of worshipers and feel the birth of a nation stirring in his loins.

The Holy Ghost

A CHRISTIAN missionary once visited the Dalai Lama intent upon converting him. He was so impressed by the radiant boy whom everyone within a thousand miles called God, however, that he came very close to renouncing his own faith and becoming a Tibetan monk. He was only able to save himself by deciding that he was in the presence of none other than the Holy Trinity – if not all three parts, at least a portion.

'Which portion?' asked the Dalai Lama.

'You're too young to be God the Father,' said the giddy missionary, 'and you lack the sense of suffering and the beard to be Jesus Christ. Surely you must be the Holy Ghost.' So saying, he fell to his knees and sang a hymn, departing only after the Dalai Lama had consented to baptize him.

Thenceforth, the Dalai Lama came to think of himself as a holy ghost. Obliterating the vibrations of his ego until he was almost invisible, he would wander through the honeycombed chambers of his palace at night when all the monks were asleep, and in many of the abandoned cells he discovered other ghosts.

He would speak to these ghosts saying, 'I am the *holy* ghost.' Soon the ghosts had fashioned themselves an invisible litter to carry their lord from room to room along corridors lit with fluttering butter lamps. A few lamas who had stayed up all night to say their beads reported seeing the Dalai Lama moving through the air in a sitting position.

Whether such reports are literally true, one cannot dispute that the Dalai Lama received from the Christian missionary a sense of his own mystery. The Tibetan word for *mystery* is also the word for *carpenter*.

Among the journals found at the bedside of the Reverend J. Cope Butterfield when he died was the following notation, which his widow sent on to the Tibetan embassy: 'Years after my visit to the Dalai Lama it has come to me that the carpenter was indeed father of our Lord.'

The Jewelled Garden

EVERY spring, the Dalai Lama left the Grand Potala and all his serene and serious rituals to spend six months at the Summer Palace, where his only duty was to keep the plants of the Jewelled Garden happy. The farmers of Tibet depended upon these particular plants to keep their lands flourishing.

So every day, the king went out to sing and dance for the plants, to stroll amongst them showering them with loving praise, to pray for them and tenderly to admonish them not to be stingy in their yields of fruit and flower.

Sooner or later, every Tibetan farmer made his pilgrimage to the Jewelled Garden there to receive a handful of seeds which, when sprouted and full grown, would become the spiritual kings and queens of the farmlands. One could look at a Tibetan field so blessed by the Dalai Lama and see that plants grew taller according to their proximity to the holy ones. Fields of barley, rice, buckwheat, maize, potatoes, turnips, onions and radishes resembled undulating mounds at harvest time, peaking wherever a seed from the Jewelled Garden had sprouted and flourished.

Indeed, the king regarded all his people as plants and his dance in the garden as harmonious with the ritual performances of the winter season at the Grand Potala, when he blessed shepherd plants and farmer plants, monk plants and merchant plants, serving plants and ruling plants.

He himself relied upon the Jewelled Garden for his

inspiration and sustenance. He had found that certain plants were sensors of his moods. He could store his better moods in various vegetables, having recourse to them whenever he could not otherwise break a period of despondency. He could, in fact, eat himself.

Just as one hangs a favorite suit in the closet to wear on special days, so when he was in a particularly loving mood he would go into the garden to hang the mood on a plant. Always open to the slightest vibrations from his presence, the chosen plant would drink the mood right up and keep it flourishing until the master felt a need of it. Then the Dalai Lama would go into his garden, pick the leaves, dry them in an oven, crush them, roll them into a dough, bake them and eat them. Soon, the loving mood would have returned.

He had planted his loving moods in rows according to their fragrance. There was a row of serenity spinach, a row of ecstasy chard, a row of bliss beans. He attempted once to cross-fertilize reverence and joviality into his rhubarb, but the rhubarb quickly wilted and died. Thenceforth, he refrained from asking his plants to absorb more than a single subtlety of fragrance at once.

Of course, the Dalai Lama was careful not to burden his plants with negative moods. These he stored elsewhere in the face of an old demoniac servant named Rampa. The Dalai Lama kicked Rampa around mercilessly when he wanted to get rid of a bad mood and could find no place else to put it. Like the faithful suffering servant that he was, the cantankerous old man would not store his bad emotions for long lest the king might have to take them back again. Instead, he would go grumbling into town each Saturday to dump them on the backs of cur dogs, bandits, syphilitic whores and other frequenters of a certain disreputable tavern. Then, stinking of vomit, he would stagger back to the palace, once more full of those pretentious poses, those false claims to grandeur that never failed to invite more of the Dalai Lama's discharge of negative energy, should such have built up in the king's system.

Movies

THERE were movies in the walls of the Potala. The Dalai Lama had only to roll his forehead against the rock and he could see figures of bygone days sitting at prayer or strolling along the corridors chanting. He could see movies in objects too.

Just as you or I might put a movie reel on a projector and look at one of our favorite actors, so the Dalai Lama could hold a favorite object, say the crusty old briar pipe Heinrich Harrer had given him, and clearly see the man who had smoked it walking his stiff-legged dog, Argos, through the alleys in the evening, stopping to chat with the lady who sold flowers, pausing to smell the aromas of breads, cakes and puddings from the bakery, frequently petting his dog, finally arriving at his friend's office just as the friend was closing up – the friend then unlocking the door and the two of them going back in to sit on either side of the desk under which the dog already had curled up asleep. Two brandy snifters were produced from a secret locked compartment on the side of the desk, the brandy was poured, the friend always said, 'Sip it,' the brandy was savored, praised, pipes were freshly lit, both men told a few stories on their wives, then a long silence. The dog began to scratch his fleas. The men began to talk philosophy.

Every time the Dalai Lama held the pipe to his forehead, the movie was the same, and he enjoyed it more each time.

He could only see movies in familiar objects used time

and again by the same person in the same way. These movies did not give a full picture of the habitual owner's life but only the reruns, the familiar routes, the oft-repeated idiosyncrasies and the general world view given off by the person's behavior and tone.

The pipe smoker's philosophy, for example (that of Harrer's grandfather who first owned the pipe), was that all real thinking is not done with the brain but with the chest. The pipe smoke is a symbolic acknowledgment of this fact − not too different from the Tibetan view that 'breath is the horse and mind is the rider.' Clearly, the old Austrian's mind was going where his chest would lead him.

The Dalai Lama had only to rub the pipe in his hands to see that the first owner's breathing region was a rustic cottage on a lake where he was alone with only his dog. He was sitting at a wooden bench in the shade of the porch with bees buzzing around the flowery vines that hung down from the roof, entirely hiding the chimney out of which smoke was slowly rising in thoughtful dreams. The old Austrian had put a permanent dream into the pipe. It showed himself rowing his leaky green boat out on the lake to a favorite spot opposite a stump in the woods on shore. He had caught a huge fish there in his boyhood and had rowed a laughing girl out to show her the magic place. In the movie, it was not the girl who sat in the back seat but the dog with its tongue hanging out. The old Austrian dreamed of himself out there on the lake smoking his pipe while a fishing line tied to an oarlock hung down, ignored, into the dark waters. The pipe smoker's philosophy had to do with uninterrupted stillness, time to meditate, the love of animals, futility of the hunt, return to the womb, and the cottage as a thought chest into which we draw all the musky aroma of our outdoor lives, hold it inside for a while, then let it out again for a visit with a friend.

While the Dalai Lama had hundreds of objects in the drawers of his desk stored with equal wealth of visual and sound vibrations from all over the world, the Austrian pipe presented as a gift by Heinrich Harrer had special significance since Harrer also had introduced the fourteen-year-old Dalai Lama to movies. This Austrian alpinist, who spent several years in Lhasa, built a projection room at the king's request with a generator made from an old car engine; also he taught the Dalai Lama how to shoot and edit his own films.

The older lamas had advised strongly against letting the Dalai Lama look at movies and Harrer had backed them all the way with this warning: 'After years of watching movies in Vienna during my youth, I came to believe that my life was nothing but a movie being watched by God and the heavenly host. I wouldn't have minded so much had I not felt that I was not one of God's favorites, that he seldom wanted to watch me and that I had been classified Grade C, to be shown only as the tail end of a triple feature every few years in some provincial heavenly village where there were only a few lovers in the back row and some dharma bums catching up on their sleep while I flickered on.'

The argument was lost on the Dalai Lama and he had his way once he pointed out how similar movies must be to the Buddhist conception of our lives as flitting appearances. The lamas insisted, however, on editing out all specifically erotic scenes, which reduced some feature-length films to as little as five minutes.

The movies had a very bad influence on the Dalai Lama, just as had been predicted. First of all, Harrer had set the projector so far back that the images were enormous, giving the Dalai Lama the impression, not to be dispelled by visits from a few Westerners, that people outside his kingdom were generally of enormous size and voice. Since spirituality in Tibet is judged by how quietly a person speaks and how small, almost invisible, he can make himself, it follows that the Dalai Lama judged the characters in these movies to be unspiritually materialistic in the extreme. He was shocked and depressed but at the same time fascinated. He would sit for days at a time watching the big movies roll on. They were not like his ephemeral psychometric visions at all. They were hard, tough pictures of hard, tough people with no poetry in their souls.

He came to see himself as a very tiny king in a sub-world of divinity – a kind of holy gremlin, genie or troll. When he learned from Harrer that his was one of the largest kingdoms in the world, he was absolutely flabbergasted. Seen from the Potala through his telescope, his people looked to him like ants. Even when he was carried into their midst, raised up on his sedan chair, they remained small and timorous in his presence. Many of the monks were big, rude, strapping fellows, and his guards were giants seven feet tall, but all these were tiny next to John Wayne, Maurice Chevalier and the others. As for the mountains, they were quaint miniatures next to the mountains of the American westerns.

Everything about the movies was terrifying. What he had thought would be the very metaphor of man's illusory, ever-changing appearance and reappearance on earth in new forms turned out to be a prophecy that matter might, after all, conquer spirit, that matter in all its nullity might become immortal while spirit gradually died away and was forgotten or stifled as Tibet might soon be by the monolith of China. The king came as close as a god can come to a mental breakdown after the movies.

The Regent kept having to remind him, 'John Wayne, too, will achieve Buddhahood, O Tender One.'

It became obvious that the Dalai Lama must make a movie to redeem all that he had seen. He made the movie and projected it one night against the outside south wall of the Potala for all the people of Lhasa to see. The film was then destroyed so that it could remain embedded in that wall for any person to enjoy who can properly press his forehead to the stones. Since the Communist invasion, nobody has seen this film, but those who remember it describe a severely edited sequence of two or three minutes during which a bird appears in the wall feather by feather until it is fully formed and ready to take flight; then, feather by feather, it flies away.

The Dalai Lama himself will only say that he never mastered the cinematographer's art but that, while studying, he regained his composure with the certain knowledge that evil is nothing but a tiny rectangle with too much light thrown upon it, an expansive gasp trapped forever in its own image, unable to grow small again and disappear. Good, on the other hand, expands and contracts, comes and goes, and is eternal.

An Eye to the West

IN the year 1950, the Chinese ambassador hurried home from Tibet to report that he had been treated most discourteously by the Dalai Lama, whom he branded as a 'bourgeois élitist with sacral pretensions.' This was one more excuse for 'saving the Tibetan people from their exploitive rulers' and has been discounted by Western historians as having no basis in fact. The Dalai Lama's uncle tells us otherwise in his article 'Occidental Causes of Oriental Tyranny.'

The king's uncle writes:

'With Westerners, my nephew was polite to a fault. On the several occasions when they caused him offense, he not only remained quiet but even allowed himself to be subjected to humiliations he never would have tolerated from his own people. He excused Westerners by saying they were innocent bunglers to be respected for their good intentions. I suspect, however, that he suffered from an inferiority complex brought on by their awesome technology.

'Westerners were always trying to get him to do something which they assured him was a harmless indulgence of their fascination with Tibet. Having given permission, he was too polite to call a stop to the horror that ensued. I have described already in my article 'God Used for Decoration' how art relics were hidden under clothing and sold in Europe as conversation pieces, when their whole purpose was to instill absolute silence in the beholder. I have described how the Dalai Lama allowed a carving of his own incarnation as Chenrezi, the Buddha of Mercy, to be photographed by a Swiss art firm, only to discover later that the art firm's junior partner had quite mercilessly carved his initials along with those of his own true love on the Buddha's back. After I gain a composed attitude on the subject, I shall describe how my nephew allowed a mass-production weaving factory to be set up by the Dutch in Tholing with a foreman who, wishing to save time, ordered an abandonment of the pause and prayer between each woven line, which is the essential mystery and vibration of Tibetan weaving, how the prayer wheels atop the looms were taken down so that the world being woven flattened itself out as if it belonged to some medieval European vision of reality ... how, finally, the weavers were told that the more they produced of a single kind of rug the less each rug would be sold for, as if there were to be no compensation at all for their tremendous compromise to boredom and repetition.

'Enough said. The reader will understand now how it was possible that the Chinese crisis was brought on by a seemingly innocent remark made to my nephew by a certain Italian woman with exquisite eyes. As this woman was passing in the receiving line to shake his hand (another indulgence of Western seizure complexes) he looked down on her and was taken aback by the beauty of her eyes. He told her that he had never seen such marvelous eyes before, they were so artistic.

' "You are not the first to tell me I have the eyes of an artist," she replied, and she went on to say that, in fact, she *was* an artist and, as such, she had admired *his* eyes also and would like to paint them.

'Seeing that her eyes had been painted with swooping black corners to ward off demons from above, purple lids to protect the powerful lights below, gold-flecked lashes, little green lines of mountains in summer, rims like brimming shorelines, pink dots at the inside folds to denote a fiery mind, he said to the lady, "I should like to have you paint my eyes."

'A time was arranged. When she arrived, he sat before her very still with his eyes closed, expecting her to start the application of paints directly to his lids and lashes. But nothing of the sort happened. When he opened his eyes at last, he saw that she was busily at work behind an easel, peeking out at him obscenely. Frightened as he was, his politeness would not allow him to move or say a word.

'He could feel something ghastly happening to his left eye. All vision was going out of it. Yet he retained his composure, believing that the dignity of his country was at stake. To keep it safe, he closed his one good eye. The other was now entirely blind.

' "Oh, don't close your eye," she cried. "When you see this one, you'll want me to paint the other one too."

'With a grunt of satisfaction, the Italian lady turned her easel around for him to see. "What do you think? Do you like it?" He couldn't see a thing, of course, and he knew he shouldn't open his one good eye, but again his manners got the better of him. What he saw made him shriek with horror.

'The guards rushed in to find him clutching his left eye. They quickly removed the lady and destroyed her painting in as merciful a manner as they could. Still, the painting left permanent scars on his cornea and damaged his optic nerve. Fortunately, one eye was spared before she could take possession of it with her brush, but months went by before my nephew could see out of it clearly again.

'Only a week after this incident, the Chinese ambassador came to extend respects from the People's Republic of

China. The head of protocol had not been informed of the king's malady and had placed the ambassador to the king's left. Alas, my nephew could not see anything in that direction, nor was he even aware of the ambassador's presence. In fact, he thought *I* was the person sitting left of him, and since he was still embarrassed by having succumbed to the Italian madwoman, he had no great desire to look at me. Finding himself totally ignored, the ambassador jumped up hastily in the middle of the meal and hurried straight back to Peking to proclaim an insult so propitious for the invasion of our country.

'So much for my nephew's so-called discourtesy to the East, which, as the reader can see, was in fact a consequence of courtesy to the West beyond the limits of safety.'

Ten Conversations at Once

EXCEPT when he was very much into the holy hum of things so that nothing could knock him off course, the Dalai Lama disliked meeting with foreigners. They obviously thought that he regarded himself as a holy man, and they insisted on treating him as such. Trying to compensate for this misapprehension on their parts, he would lean over backward to be casual, to make small talk, to show that he could be as common, superficial and even vulgar as the next fellow. Since he was none of these any more than he was a holy man, he would chastise himself for putting on a phony hail-fellow-well-met act during visits, especially from Europeans.

After a visit with Europeans, the inner soliloquy which every good Buddhist hopes to be rid of once and for all would start up again, generated by the nagging question, Why do I always look for postures with these people?

Because when I start just being myself they start treating me with some kind of phony reverence. When I start being real, they start being phony, so I try to get phony to make them real. It's a lost cause. Why do I bother? They don't think I'm holy any more than I do. In fact, they probably think they're much holier than I am but that if they reveal this they'll be insulting Tibetan customs. So, to hide their self-esteem, they pretend to think me holier than they, confident that I'll go along with the game, since I undoubtedly have the same opinion of myself. In fact, I couldn't possibly have this opinion of myself, could I, since no holy man ever consciously thinks of himself as such. Ah me, it's hard to be myself with foreigners. I must avoid them.

Troubled by such ruminations and by the fact that even a number of people in his own country suffered under the delusion that he was the holiest among them, he went to the roof of the Potala and up the ladder to the highest golden-domed cell, where lived the lama whom he considered holiest of all. This lama, who was called Great Hum, was no mere official incarnation of God. Tibet would never have wasted him on ceremonial functions. He was much more than a sacred symbol trying diligently to become its own reality. The Great Hum *was* his own reality. He was neither more nor less than himself, neither happier nor sadder than himself, wiser nor more foolish than himself. He was exactly what he was.

There was no need for the Great Hum to change expressions on his face since a single expression could allow all moods to flow from it. Seriousness and humour, light and darkness, soul and spirit were all united in the evenness of his gaze. He could smile without moving his lips. Just when you thought his eyes were full of amusement, you would realize how utterly sad they were; and when you thought the sadness was on the verge of moving him to tears, you would perceive that he was feeling no deep emotions whatsoever but was only watching you with calm, purely intellectual curiosity, and when you had this perception well in mind so that you felt prepared to provide him with some detached answers to whatever questions he might wish to ask, it would dawn on you that he could not possibly be curious since he was all-knowing and there was nothing left for him to be curious about. Whether such omniscience made him supremely indifferent or passionately concerned was impossible to tell.

Finally you gave up trying to decipher the Great Hum's expression and you began to project your own feelings upon him. He absorbed these in a comforting way, letting his face appear as the image not of what you were but of what you would become if you continued on your present course – a realization that made you change your course with haste until you had given up desiring every stance in life that you could imagine as being desirable. You were left with no feelings for him to reflect, at which time his face would begin to withdraw from you into a kind of shadow until you could only see the vague slit where his mouth had been. The face would stay hidden, causing you to fear that it might disappear altogether without satisfying the absolute necessity you now felt for conversation with it. When you were entirely possessed by this sense of necessity, you would hear him start to hum and you would realize that he had been humming all along. Then he would emerge from his shadow. The hum would break down into words and he would be speaking to you without ever opening his mouth.

This most holy of the teaching lamas was noted more sensationally for being able to carry on ten conversations at once. In his golden tower, he held audience for an hour every evening. He would sit facing the ten visitors, looking at none of them yet looking at them all by looking inward and finding them there within himself as he saw them struggling with the dilemmas they had brought to him. It was said of him that just as the ocean can dissolve into a drop of water so all men can dissolve into the Great Hum.

The Dalai Lama climbed the ladder and entered the dome of this same Great Hum. Already five others had seated themselves. One of these was a highly developed lama who could sing three notes at once, each note carrying a different conversation. Another could carry on two conversations and the other three could carry on only one. This meant that eight conversations were already taking place. Since the Dalai Lama could carry on two, his arrival completed the number of visitors allowed and he closed the door after him.

The golden dome was like a beehive, for all the conversations consisted of humming. Words were superfluous.

The humming of the Dalai Lama sounded more like a groan. It went something like this: 'I accuse myself of being a fakir who tricks people into seeing God with faces that are nothing but grotesque masks. I'm afraid that my father might get drunk one night and give away the trick. Then all the people of Tibet will know that I'm not God, and the country will fall into despair. I try to let them know that I'm only a boy from the country with a certain amount of religious education and a lucky streak that won him the throne. But they insist on treating my act as a reality. The more I try to act like I'm not holy, the more holy everybody thinks I am.'

'The magicians and the storytellers,' answered the Great Hum, 'open us up to wonder with their tricks. We are lured into the eternal reality by well-timed illusion, for illusions appear as enticing emanations from around that oval into which faces vanish when ego surrenders to the mystifying Self. Great are those actors who can put people on and take people off. You accuse yourself of being two-faced. Look at me.'

The Great Hum was transforming himself into an old woman, a beautiful girl, a fierce warrior, a child ... yet the voice remained the same as it went on to say, 'Once you're free from bondage to your face, you'll be able to take on as many faces as you like – not just two or three but a thousand. The more faces you assume, the more your expression will remain the same. Eventually, when you try to resemble me, as you are doing now, you will find that I have come to resemble you instead. But you have much to learn before then. You are faced with contradictory feelings about your role and will remain so until you can assume any mask the world places upon you and wear it with ease. Only then will your own divine countenance shine through. Are you not a god? Do the gods not wear masks?'

While one of the Dalai Lama's voices was talking to the Great Hum about faces, the other was talking about voices. 'My top voice,' said the boy king, 'is very cultured and polite. It serves to hide the sensitivities that I need to protect. This voice keeps the silence secret, screens my meditating self from the petty and persistent interruptions of curiosity seekers. My lower voice has to do with the powerful bottom desires and the private urges to become a bodhisattva.'

'Quite right,' said the Great Hum. 'Religious ceremonials should be surrounded by clowns. The mask must do parodies of the face beneath it, lest the sacred be profaned and the immortal confound itself with mortality. There's an old saying about the public domain: "If you're going to do anything serious, make sure you've got the tourists laughing; and when they stop laughing let the humor begin." Have you heard any good stories lately? The old monk on your left has been telling me two funny stories at once while his middle voice whispers about God.'

The Dalai Lama was embarrassed. He could not think of a single funny story to tell the Great Hum. 'Wisest of Us All,' he murmured, 'forgive me, for I can think of nothing that would make you laugh.'

'I'm laughing already,' said the Great Hum, 'so relax. I've been laughing ever since you came in. So much of what you talk about is pure clowning. I know that one of your voices is down in the chapel talking to God, but the louder one is up here on the roof playing games with virtuoso religious ideas and amusing itself with psychological analyses of its ambiguous self. I know that your voice cares only to keep the seasons changing and the world from blowing up. It cares nothing for how many faces or voices it has but only for the continuing beauty of the cosmos. Unless you perfect your style, few people will hear this voice. Try on all the masks you like, speak in as many voices as you can. Someday you'll be able to carry on ten conversations at once just as I do. Then you can come up here all alone and we can talk face to face, voice to voice, one to one, a single presence with nothing to hide.'

It came to the Dalai Lama as he climbed back down the ladder that a single voice can be heard in ten different ways when it responds to ten different conditions, and he remembered once when the spirit of a famous guru appeared to heal a small, discordant community of monks. All the monks had seen the spirit come out of the wall long enough to utter just one word. But each monk had heard a different word. The event is immortalized in this poem:

> The one who wanted to die heard *live*.
> The one who wanted to live heard *die*.
> The one who wanted to take heard *give*.
> The one who wanted to give heard *keep*.
> The one who was always alert heard *sleep*.
> The one who was always asleep heard *wake*.
> The one who wanted to leave heard *stay*.
> The one who wanted to stay, *depart*.
> The one who never spoke heard *preach*.
> The one who always preached heard *pray*.
> Each one learned how he had been
> In someone else's way.

The Phantom Lover

The poems of the sixth Dalai Lama give perfect expression to the poet's yearning for love. I was not the only person to appreciate the verses of this lonely prisoner: many Tibetans love the poems of their long-dead ruler. He was an original figure in the line of the Dalai Lamas. He loved women and used to disguise himself and slip into town to meet them. His people did not begrudge him his desire to satisfy the needs of his poetic soul.

— Heinrich Harrer

FOR hundreds of years a story gossiped in the market-places concerned the sixth Dalai Lama. It seems that a young woman caught in sin was brought to the sixth Dalai Lama for judgment. Her sin was so outrageous that the Regent, who ordinarily enforced the laws, felt himself incapable of devising a punishment severe enough to fit the crime. She had been caught by her father having intercourse with a yak.

But this was not the worst, since the father had not witnessed this scene alone. When he surprised his daughter behind the sheepfold, he had found a number of other animals, wild and domestic, waiting their turns in states of excitement.

The sixth Dalai Lama took one look at the young woman and, like the yak, the dog, the tiger and the goat, he too was filled with such longing for her that he asked the Regent to leave the room. The young woman then knelt before her god and king, and looked up into his face with what is called in Tibet the Sunbeam Smile.

She was smiling with erotic compassion, for she could see the perpetually sad yearning for bliss in the beautiful eyes of the king. She could see him as the eager monkey of his earliest incarnation when he created the people of Tibet. She told him how her dog and her horse had begun to show signs of desiring her and how, finally, her love for them became so great that she could refuse them no longer. As a consequence, it came to pass that animals were following her wherever she went, coming down from the mountains and up from the forests and streams.

The whole creation seemed to be yearning for her and she, in turn, yearned so passionately to satisfy it that she had finally opened herself without reserve to any creature that wished to enter her body or warm itself at her breast. Yet no creature could satisfy her entirely.

She told her story happily and without remorse, and when she had fallen silent to await her punishment the sixth Dalai Lama said to himself: This is no common scandal. She is the scandal of creation itself. If she can give herself so gladly to all the sexual longings on earth, then her partner in sin must be God. I, being God, have sinned with her, for these animals were nothing but manifestations of myself.

To the young woman, he said, 'Rise and rejoice. Your sins are no sins at all since they were committed for my sake. Your only punishment is that you shall be satisfied.'

After he had judged her to their mutual satisfaction, he called in the Regent. 'I have found this woman innocent of sin,' he said. 'I find that she is filled only with the sweetest and most liquid longings to satisfy nature's eagerness. I hereby appoint her Mother Superior of the Order of Temple Virgins. May all that she has received from the

animal world serve to attract and elevate the longings of men. And may she be opened now to the eagerness of the cosmos.'

Of all his previous incarnations, his sixth interested the Dalai Lama most of all. Thanks to this sixth presence, no man in Tibet ever suffered sexual frustrations; for, be he ugly, deformed, senile or pubescent, he had only to travel to a village where he was a stranger and knock on any door with a request for sexual relief to be welcomed by the women as if he were the most attractive man on earth.

Nor would any man of the house object if the stranger asked to make love to his wife or daughter. On the contrary, he would hardly be able to keep his delight within the limits of decorum, so thrilled would he feel that the visitor might just possibly be the Dalai Lama in disguise. Readily giving over his woman and bed, he would retire to another room there to kneel excitedly with ear pressed to the wall, in hopes of catching the cry signifying that the seed might have been planted just then, in his very house, in his very woman, by God Himself ... The seed of the new king incarnate.

As for the woman, her joy at being ravished by a stranger knew no bounds. She would go to every excess to satisfy him as marvelously as she could. Everyone knew how the poet king liked to take on repulsive disguises in order to test the blind faith of the women he made love to. He assumed that a woman would recognize him, no matter how he appeared, by the divine intensity of his ardor and by the abandon of her spirit to him. And the women weren't taking any chances.

All this expectation of a divine visit kept Tibetan men very satisfied with their wives. A man would make sure that his woman was erotically in tune by saying to her,

'Prepare yourself radiantly, dearest, for tonight the God-King may come down from the Grand Potala to hold you in his arms.' Thus, every woman was as ready for her man as she would have been for the Holy Ghost.

The people assumed that the fourteenth Dalai Lama had not changed from incarnation to incarnation and that he still snuck down into the villages in disguise to visit their women. This was wishful thinking, however, since his most recent presence was a shy young man who remained strictly faithful to his celibate vows. True, the fourteenth loved the sixth best of all his prior lives, but he understood that poetic self the least and feared his manner of death most of all, since the sixth Dalai Lama had suffered a year's agony from slow poison dropped into his cup by one of those crusader monks who appear now and then in every country to purify mankind of excess happiness.

The memoirs of the sixth God-King were carved in birch-wood boards bound with silk, which only the new incarnations were allowed to untie and read. They contained such passages as these:

They say much is to be forgiven me, for I love women. I forgive them much for saying so.

So many sweet cunts. Each petal opens inside of me like a slow wound.

Here I am in the palace writing love poems to the latest of my filthy women and planning another sortie to have a go at her mother. The Regent tells me I should repent before I become one of the demons in my chamber of horrors. Doesn't he know I'm meeting evil on its own terms, doing battle with lust by lusting? Doesn't he know the demons are all Buddhas in disguise? Yes, I'm grotesque. I go through my contortions with women squirming and screaming for mercy beneath me. But these are the playful screams of pleasure. They know that when I spray them with my power I'm emptying myself so that God might be purified.

How sweet were the vows of celibacy until the Crusader Monk soured them with guilt. Praised be the power that shaped my will and praised be the power that broke it, for when law comes without love, let love take a stealthy leave. I have no choice. So long as he roams the countryside preaching that free union between men and women is evil, I must save our men and women from poisoning of the flesh.

Be it known that my people were born of my lust. I changed myself into a monkey and ravished the demoness for their sakes. Everything I have done since then has been for their sakes. I am the Buddha of Mercy. I am the hairy incarnation of a wooing god. At night, I disguise myself in the clothing of a yak driver and sneak into Lhasa to ravage the women. Tibet is being born through me. Filthy women, panting in your dark places for my arrival, my poems are for you. How we stank as we fucked!

The fourteenth Dalai Lama read these and other memoirs of his sixth presence with mixed envy and dread. Long ago he had known his creation through direct sensual contact. Now he gleaned whatever information he could from the limited angle of vision afforded by his telescope. Everything was seen from above, as in a Chinese painting. Even when he traveled, he was on a litter.

Once, he was called before a friendly tribunal to explain why he had broken his celibate vows so long ago. Had he not realized that he was androgynous, without need of sexual relations with anyone else? Did he not know that he was his own lover and that he need never make love to anyone except an extension of his own imagination? A few of the lamas suggested coyly that perhaps his sixth presence had been merely a front man for the true Dalai Lama who had stayed in meditative seclusion to escape the intrigues of the Crusader Monk. Wanly, the Dalai Lama admitted that it might have been so and asked the assemblage to excuse him.

That night, when the moon was full, he mounted to the roof of the Potala. He was wearing the mask of a beautiful girl. On twisted strands of his own hair were hung diminutive figures of himself in all the male and female aspects of his office. He had carved these from the tusks of the two beloved elephants who had taught him the enormous beauty and tenderness of sexuality. He jumped up on the ramparts and danced for his people who were watching from the steps of the Potala far below, where they had gathered to celebrate his existence. They too began to dance. He spun and they spun until all were dizzy, then they let out a gasp. The drums stopped rolling. They saw him teeter and almost fall toward them before he regained his balance and jumped back down to the roof. Laughing with relief, they danced on.

The Dalai Lama put one of his necklace carvings in his mouth and tasted once more the groans of an elephant dying of love. The people were as close to his palace as he had been to the elephants before they died. It was not unknown for a pilgrim to die of love for him after a long journey just as one elephant had died for the other. Could he ever die of love? he wondered. He wished that he could. But he had been taught above all to love himself, and how can one die of self-love? If only the man in him could find a woman in him to teach him to love himself more. They said he was both male and female, but through the woman's mask he remained a man, lonely for the half he could not find.

He took off his mask and looked through his telescope at the jubilant crowd, conscious that he too was being viewed through a hole in the celestial dome by a cosmic voyeur whose Potala was the earth itself. The Dalai Lama raised his telescope just in time to see this God above God become a goddess, her milky legs spread across the heavens with clouds wafting across her full moon like curling hair. He put on his woman's mask again.

Once more, God became a man with a long telescope, watching from above. When the boy opened his mouth to say 'O,' God answered with a hum, and when God hummed, the Dalai Lama's mouth opened round and he became God's daughter quivering for the entry of the holy spirit. O entered M. wOMan.

'O!' he cried. 'O! Om!'

Pyramid Lake

The Regent had assured the Dalai Lama that the cold shivers he so often experienced while performing the high rituals of his office would trouble him no more once he had matured to his Godhood. But the king could not imagine a time when he would entirely warm to the presumption of letting himself be adored; and body heat such as certain others in his kingdom were capable of astounded him.

One young monk, for example, had proved his mastery over all the others by standing naked on the ice of Pyramid Lake until it melted under his feet and he sank through into the water. This same monk had dipped forty shirts into the water and dried them one after the other upon his body. He was then given the official title, Hot Monk of Tibet.

This hottest of monks was sent for by the Dalai Lama and asked to serve as a secret guide for the king's pilgrimage to Pyramid Lake on the occasion of his ninth year on the throne.

The Hot Monk and the Dalai Lama journeyed to Pyramid Lake disguised as herdsmen. The lake was in the arid desert country of the high central plateau, surrounded by sandy wastes and sparse grasses. The white island a mile offshore was said to be visited by mysterious black birds who arrived only at night to visit their nests and leave before sunrise. No one had actually seen these birds, though their shadows reflected on the still water were sometimes glimpsed on moonlit nights by the ferrymen, who are responsible for the saying, 'Living forms are as fleeting as the shadows of nightbirds on Pyramid Lake.' (In Tibetan, the words for *shadow* and *reflection* are the same.) The existence of these birds could be verified by the huge nests covering the rocky island as thickly as monk cells in a lamasery. There was speculation that the birds were all male since no eggs had ever been found.

Pyramid Lake is perhaps the most sacred lake in Tibet. At an elevation of more than fifteen thousand feet, its water is faintly saline, as if it had been lifted up by the mountains when they sprang from the sea. Schools of huge royal trout swim in its waters which remain frozen at one end while staying always warm at the other, due to the continuous inflow from streams originating in geysers and hot springs that gush, burst and bubble from the mineral-encrusted terrain nearby.

The clear, hot water from these springs winds toward the lake in numerous rivulets, whose mushy banks and bottoms can be dammed up and hollowed out to form baths where people from all over Tibet come to cure diseases of the skin and bone and to erase the wrinkles accumulated from squinting into the wind while smiling.

Dry mud from Pyramid Lake is sold as a healing balm in the Tibetan marketplaces and is used by the Dalai Lama to maintain his smooth and serene complexion.

The Dalai Lama had long wanted to go to the place where this mud came from, but tradition allowed only that he go there on his ninth year in power, to reenact symbolically what once had been an actual ritual of death, burial and rebirth. Before Buddhism reached Tibet from India more than a thousand years ago, the king of Tibet had been allowed to rule for only nine years, after which time he was taken by his people to the warm banks of Pyramid Lake, where a shallow trough was dug for him in the hot mud. When it had filled with water, he would quite happily give himself over to the high priest, who would immerse him, holding him under until he had drowned. The water would then be allowed to drain into the lake and the king would be buried in the mud.

It was believed that he would enter into the earth mother's womb, there to be kept for nine months, after which time he would slither out as a royal trout. This earth mother was called the Great Mud Sow and was the very ancestor of the Great Sow who now governed all the nuns of Tibet.

Pyramid Lake was believed to be filled with the ancient kings of Tibet reborn from the belly of the Great Mud Sow as trout.

After Buddhism, the death and rebirth ritual was reduced to mere symbology. Mud from the hot springs near the lake would be brought to the Dalai Lama so that he could rub it daily on his face. On his ninth year in power, he would journey to Pyramid Lake to reenact the ritual, no longer taking a large retinue but going in disguise with only a single attendant.

The king and his guide arrived at the warm end of the lake near sunset. The Hot Monk set about making camp at the base of some huge pink sandstone rocks two and three hundred feet high, which the wind had carved into the likenesses of voluptuous figures embracing. Eager bellies, breasts and buttocks bulged from these rocks while all around could be heard the gurgling of water as it burst from underground onto the slimy, lime-covered plain.

A geyser occasionally hissed nearby, erupting and echoing against the rocks until the passionate stone lovers seemed to shudder in orgasm. Across the nearby ground,

steam arose from hot rivulets that snaked toward the lake
and finally spilled into its belly.

The Hot Monk had carried firewood with him and now
a campfire was blazing. He and the Dalai Lama sat down
to seek guidance in the flames. Presently, the king felt overwhelmed by the familiar chillness that came over him
whenever he was too intensely adored.

'Dear brother Hot Monk,' he said humbly, 'I want you to
forget that I'm your god and king and I want you to confide
in me as the admiring friend that I am. You, more than
anyone else, understand the fire within us and how to
express its power. Tell me what this power consists of.'

The Hot Monk extended his arms slowly into the fire,
grasped a flaming stick and swallowed its flame. He smiled
shyly. 'Alas, it's only a trick of the mind, Your Highness.
Some people can make the water in their bodies pour out
until they're nothing but shrunken skin on dry bone.
Others can make birds fly from their sleeves. Others can
produce beautiful stones from their bowels. Fire, water,
stone, birds: we are all of these and we can turn one into
the other, but we cannot create elements from nothing. You
alone are capable of this. You create elements, I merely
rearrange them. I'm a trickster hungering for God. You
are God and hunger for nothing. Unceasing hunger, my
Lord, never leaves us mortals in peace until we ourselves are
consumed by a hunger stronger than ours. Isn't it so?'

The Dalai Lama never could get over his amazement that
men such as this monk, who had advanced so much further
than he, could still believe that he was any more of a god
than they, and that he not only knew the answer to their
questions but that he *was* the answer.

'Who do you say that I am?' the twelve-year-old Dalai
Lama asked the twenty-one-year-old monk.

'You are my father.'

'And who is *my* father?'

The Hot Monk laughed. 'You are your own father, Sire.'

'And am I my own mother, too?'

'Your mother is over there waiting for you, Your Highness.' He pointed toward the steaming fields near the bank of the lake. 'I give thanks to you, O God, for choosing me to assist at your death and resurrection.'

The Dalai Lama yearned to feel within himself the holiness attributed to him. 'Do you think I shall be changed when I come out of the mud?'

'They say that when you come out spring changes to summer in the hearts of our people, for you cease to appear as a boy and appear as a man.'

'Let us see,' said the Dalai Lama rising.

The Hot Monk took a flaming branch and led the king to one of the hot streams. Where the stream reached the edge of the lake, he dammed it up until there was a pool deep enough to lie in. The Dalai Lama removed his robe and entered the water as it spilled over the lip of the pool into the lake. His companion sat down on the ground.

Gradually the distant fire died out.

They watched the tip of a crescent moon appear like a shining mountain peak across the water. The moon rose and lit the lake so brightly that the golden backs of the ancient Tibetan kings could be seen flashing on the surface. Far away, the white island where the birds were said to nest waxed and waned like the inside of a butter lamp.

When the Dalai Lama could bear the heat no longer, he stood up to enjoy the breeze upon his flesh. The Hot Monk began to smear him with smooth mud from the bottom of the pool. He covered the God-King thickly from head to foot, leaving openings only for his mouth and eyes. Even his ears and nose were stuffed with mud so that he could neither hear nor smell nor feel warmth or cold. The lake was very still.

As the clay hardened on his body, the Dalai Lama stood facing the shimmering lake. The water became still as a mirror. His skin was being drawn tight. The tighter it became, the more he longed to break loose and fly. An air sign, summoned to the sky, he was an infant again, strapped to his mother's back. They were out in the fields watching his older sisters and brother fly their kites. Now he saw over the pyramid-shaped island huge black kites fluttering like birds. And the island was the whitewashed Potala as he had last seen it while rounding a mountain pass into Lhasa.

'Mother!' he cried. 'The kites!'

His mother squealed like a sow with delight. The kites were moving toward them. They had stopped circling the island and were flying in a line across the water directly aimed for the place where mother and infant watched.

Now he was a rocky statue. He felt the wind from their black wings shearing the loose sand from his shoulders. The birds struck his breast like wads of mud.

The Hot Monk was slapping more clay upon the Dalai Lama's body. Motionless, he stood watching the moon move across the sky and disappear as light spread its aura upon the distant mountains. The birds were inside him now, nesting in his shoulders, chest and groin. They were flying through his veins, fluttering in his hands. But they were swimming, too, like fish or flames streaking in shoals through the watery air that flowed over his eyes.

If only he could lift his arms, he would be able to fly away to his island palace and settle once more upon his throne of straw. He fell backward into the water and dissolved.

When the mud had all washed away, he knew from the reflection in the eyes of the Hot Monk bending down gazing at him that he had been unified in permanent astonishment to all the elements and that his manhood was upon him as an awareness that he was no longer watching the mystery. He *was* the mystery. He *was* the pyramid, the lake, the mud, the birds, the god and king – all elements joined in one form.

He studied the face of the Hot Monk to see whether his companion understood this too about himself. But it was clear that this radiant person still believed God was God and man was man. Filled with an uncomprehending appreciation of the enigma that separated them, he threw his arms around the Hot Monk. 'Don't you see, there's nothing that separates us?' he said warmly. 'Doesn't this place tell you that?'

'Alas,' replied the Hot Monk, 'I'm but a trickster. I only understand the way, not the place.'

The Gasp of Amazement

IT was the custom for monks to gather on the steps of the
Potala to question each other on matters of theology. Each
would have his turn to stand before the others while being
presented with a riddle. His answer invariably brought
gasps of amazement. The questions were always the same
and so were the answers, memorized from a time long forgotten when they were first asked and answered by highly
original lamas greater than any lama today presumed he
could ever be (since it was believed that the world was running down).

The Dalai Lama, much to his distress, was not exempt
from these inquisitions. Once a year he was required to
stand before the assembled monks and lamas to go through
an act that he detested. Someone chosen by lot to ask a
single question planted by the Dalai Lama's tutors ahead
of time would stand up and, with pretense of a great mental
struggle to find just the right words, would finally blurt
out the riddle which the Dalai Lama, having carefully prepared himself for, would answer after a pregnant pause.
Then everyone would gasp with amazement.

Runners would fly to the four corners of the kingdom to
announce along trails and in the marketplaces that the boy
king had astonished one and all with the profundity of his
answer, proving once more that he was the true God and
that all was well in Tibet.

The Dalai Lama put up with this until the age of

thirteen, when a deep melancholy overcame him as he was preparing for the next interrogation. He began to dread the gasp of amazement that would ensue from his rote answer to a question neither he nor his tutors could really understand, even though he had learned the vibration of each word in the answer so well that he could make a clay pot crack in two just by saying it aloud.

The question: How do the rivers answer a bird when it rains?

The answer: By turning to snow.

He began to wish that he could just once give an answer that would silence forever the gasp of amazement, penetrating the veil of ritual courtesy to enter the living mind. He longed to say something that would leave the monks sitting there on the steps in the sunshine with their mouths hanging open and their breaths stopped short. But what could he say?

He worried and he wondered, wondered and worried, pacing the roofs of the Potala. The more he tried to think of a profound answer, the more wrinkled his brow became, the more gnarled his brain became, the more sunken his eyes became, the more uneven his breath became. But, despite a sudden aging that transformed his appearance from boy to old man in a few weeks, he could not come up with the astonishing answer he so desired, and increasingly he dreaded the day of the gasp of amazement.

Early on the appointed day he summoned the Regent to his room. Upon entering, the Regent let out a gasp of amazement. Before him stood a wizened old man on whose weary face could plainly be seen the despair of a god who has answered the same question a million times without ever yet being understood by men.

The Regent could see how the image of God had somehow become imprisoned in a withered skin wrapped in

96

celestial trappings and hung with a dusty rosary. The god of pure duration and continuous change had moved on, leaving behind this old relic of an avatar, despondent, reduced to being a mere symbol, robbed of his creativeness.

'There will be no more official amazement in our kingdom,' croaked the old king. 'We will start using our minds again. Tell them I want a new question simply put, something that won't amaze me but will make me more aware of what the conditions of life on earth really are. Tell them I absolutely forbid them to gasp at my answer.'

When the decrepit, shriveled-up remnant of the Dalai Lama appeared at high noon before the eight thousand monks of the Potala, they all gasped inwardly to see what had happened to their dear boy, but outwardly they managed to remain composed. Not a single monk could find a new question to ask until long after the sun had set and the stars were like flashing ice in the midnight air.

Finally a voice from one of the younger monks could be heard to ask timidly, 'Aren't you cold, my king? Hadn't you better go inside?'

'Yes, I'm cold,' said the Dalai Lama. 'Aren't we all?'

All said, 'Yes, Lord, we are.'

And he said, 'Then let us go inside.'

When all had assembled in the ceremonial hall and the thousands of butter lamps were fluttering warmly, the king was seen to ascend his throne. Already he looked much younger. And by the time he had said, 'That's the kind of question we should ask each other and that's the kind of answer we should give,' he had become their boy again, grinning from ear to ear.

The Decompensator of Lhasa

ONE of the Dalai Lama's best friends was a millionaire holy man named Klune, who traveled the world dressed in yachting clothes holding seminars for wealthy people – mostly old ladies – who rewarded him well for what they believed to be his inexhaustible wealth of spiritual wisdom. His kind of wealth seemed fair exchange for theirs. Dr Klune admitted to the Dalai Lama in a moment of candor that he had honed his wisdom down to a single phrase – 'All is compensation' – which he repeated no matter what problem was brought to him. Without fail the suppliant would go away grateful and radiant in the conviction that ultimate truth had been revealed at last. Whether the problem was lust, hate, guilt, jealousy, desire or pride, the solution was to give it up as mere compensation. And if the problem was excessive wealth, there was no harm in decompensating oneself to Dr Klune, who could use it wisely, precisely because he did not need it.

Klune confessed to the Dalai Lama that he always knew the answer he was going to give before he heard the question, therefore his time was free to wander off in dreams even when he was surrounded by vast crowds. The Dalai Lama realized that he and his friend were opposites. 'I never phrase my advice the same way twice,' he told Dr Klune. To which Klune replied: 'The more it's the same, the more it changes. Every new word of advice is but compensation for the inadequacy of the word that came before.'

The Dalai Lama was always glad when Klune was around to throw new perspective on his thoughts. It was Klune who provided the Dalai Lama with the monk who was to collect more gifts for the royal treasury than any other person in the history of Tibet. Without Klune's guidance, the king would have thrown this same monk into prison.

Here is what happened.

In order to avoid mutual embarrassment, people in the holy city were accustomed to taking from each other without asking. When a man and wife visited friends, they would bring a ceremonial gift, usually a scarf or pot of butter. The master of the house would accept this by replying, 'Everything we have is yours. When you leave, please take whatever you need. Take this, for example.' And he would designate the most valuable object in the house. The couple would express their thanks and all would sit down to tea.

Later, when the wife of the host had gone to fetch something from outside and the men were deep in conversation, the visiting wife would wander around the house until she came upon some little thing she really could use at home. Then, with a giggle that signaled any children present to look discreetly away, she would hide the object in the ample folds of her dress. In this way, she would not have embarrassed her hosts by taking less than they would have felt obliged to give, and she would not have embarrassed herself by discussing the petty nature of her needs.

When the very objects of highest value which friends had been offering each other for years, with complete confidence that these would never actually be taken, began to disappear – objects of gold, bronze and fine bone china – the owners were shocked and deeply hurt. For some time each injured family hid its grievances, but friendships became so strained that finally nobody was visiting anybody else. Social life had come to a grudging standstill.

Yet objects of value continued to disappear.

Before long, every well-to-do home in Lhasa had been emptied of the treasure it most esteemed. Finally, it dawned on these good people, to whom robbery had long been unthinkable, that a stealer and not merely an obnoxious taker was at work in Lhasa.

Roadblocks were set up at all exits from the city, but the thievery continued while none of the loot was found. A door-to-door search was carried out, also without success. The city elders came to a very embarrassing conclusion. Since all homes in Lhasa are guarded by dogs who viciously attack anyone intent upon causing physical or emotional suffering to the residents, and since these dogs of infallible instinct had slumbered peacefully throughout the periods of theft, it followed that the thief must have come and gone with the best intentions; that he was, in fact, removing the valuables so that they might serve some higher good aimed at enhancing the lives of the victims. Perhaps it was his way of chiding them for offering what they never really intended to give.

An assembly of all the victims was called, at which prayers of thanksgiving were offered to the unknown thief for showing them their hypocrisy. They resolved from now on to offer their guests only those articles with which they would truly be glad to part.

This new custom, alas, did not end the robberies. The elders were forced to conclude that the trouble came from above. One of the numerous lamas who descended regularly from the Potala to move freely through the houses chasing away evil spirits must be the culprit. They sent a delegation to the Dalai Lama asking him to conduct an investigation.

The Dalai Lama flatly refused and dismissed the delegation with a stern reprimand. He had second thoughts, however, when he reached for his telescope one afternoon while having tea with Dr Klune to discover that it had vanished from the place where he always laid down this favorite toy. The servants were unable to find it. Not since someone had removed the insignia from the thirteenth Dalai Lama's Stutz Bearcat had anyone dared appropriate the king's own property. The boy was enraged.

'Search every cell in this palace,' he cried.

'I wouldn't do that if I were you,' warned Dr Klune. 'You'll only humiliate your monks and unsettle the sense of trust so essential to community.'

The holy man was right. Nothing but beads and bowls were found in any cell, and several of the indignant lamas were departing for other monasteries. The king and his friend watched their procession from the balcony. One much-loved lama even looked up, then spat on the ground before hurrying after the others.

'What shall I do?' cried the Dalai Lama.

'My dear king,' said Dr Klune, 'if I were you I would search your royal treasury.'

'You think someone's even gone into my treasury?' asked the king, blanching. 'Unthinkable. Not in the whole history of Tibet has anyone entered those rooms to take what was received only so that the givers might gain. Even though the treasure belongs to me, not even I would dare touch it.'

'Nevertheless, I suggest we take a look,' Klune insisted.

So they went down the hundreds of winding stairs to the dungeon where gifts to the king were stored for eternity. Valuable objects of every kind had been stuffed into seemingly endless rooms. Golden plates, lamps and figurines had tumbled out of the arches to clutter the hallways. The Keeper of the Royal Hoard, a sleepy old lama,

held his lamp high, leading them over the debris toward
the room that was presently being filled. There, on top of
the pile, the Dalai Lama was astonished to see his own telescope, and all around he recognized objects recently stolen
from the townspeople.

'How did this come here!' he demanded.

'It was brought down by the young Collector of the
Hoard,' said the bewildered old lama. 'That nice young
monk, what's-his-name—'

'Send him to me at once.'

The king and Dr Klune were back on the roof at tea
when the offender arrived. To the Dalai Lama's surprise,
this radiantly handsome young monk, so highly respected
that he had been placed in charge of collecting gifts and
carrying them to the treasury, entered beaming with pleasure and threw himself at Dr Klune's feet, kissing the cuffs
of the holy man's white flannel trousers.

'You know this traitor?' asked the king.

'Never met him before in my life,' said Dr Klune, quite
taken aback. 'Stand up, boy. Really, this is no way to act.
Explain yourself.'

But the monk continued to humble himself, wetting the
holy man's canvas yachting shoes with his tears until
finally one of the palace guards forced him to stand. 'Good
master Klune,' sobbed the boy most joyously, 'I never
dreamed I would have the luck to meet you face to face.'

Klune blushed, glancing at the king. 'I was afraid of this,
Your Highness. What we have here, no doubt, is one of
my converts gone a bit amok. This happens more than I like
to admit, and I do regret the difficulties I've indirectly
caused. More and more, you see, through no wish of my
own, my teachings seem to be getting out of hand among
the young. Carried away by their contempt for people's
attachment to their belongings, they have taken to

decompensating them unmercifully. Robbing them, in fact. What am I to do when the youth of certain countries where I have had influence instigates a regular crime wave in behalf of my theories of nonattachment? Though I cannot renounce my beliefs, this while distortion of my intent has led me to considering retirement. In recent years, my usual audience of harmless ladies has been supplemented by greater and greater contingents of vagrant young absolutists chafing against the acquisitiveness even of certain cities in your land. This boy, no doubt, comes from among these.'

'You mean to tell me –?'

'Precisely, Highness. Correct me if I'm wrong, young man, but during the time that you were wandering with your begging bowl, did you not hear me lecture? Yes, I thought so. And did I not cause you to become horrified by the thought of so many people condemned to misery because of their wealth? Yes, indeed. And did you then not decide to devote your life to religious thievery?'

The boy was nodding constantly, grateful to be so understood.

'And when you looked at the goods you had planned to bury or destroy, did you not realize that, while these had been used for vain and unworthy purposes, they had nevertheless been created by artisans purely for the celebration of that beauty which is divine?'

The monk affirmed that it was so.

'And you contrived to become the treasurer's assistant, did you not, so that the articles stolen might be hidden and preserved for the glory of the God and King who sits in judgment on you now?'

'Yes, master!' cried the monk, and he flung himself once more at Dr Klune's feet.

'*Voilà*, Your Highness!' said the holy man. 'It is explained. I must apologize for creating, against my will, a holy thief. I shall leave you now so that you may pass judgment without interference from me.' Extricating his legs from the monk's embrace, he rose and retired to his room.

When the monk dared look up, he saw that the eyes of the Dalai Lama were filled with affection. 'Fellow seeker,' said the king gently, 'you must humbly return what you have taken, for you cannot put aside another man's burden for him. Whatever burden a man puts into God's treasury so that he might shed the weight that prevents him from rising must be put there through his own choice. As a penance, I set you this task: to find a way of returning each object stolen with such abundance of love for the owner that he shall offer it again without misgiving to our care. When this is accomplished, you shall become the new Keeper of the Royal Hoard.

'And to show you that your zeal is not without power to persuade, I am giving you my beloved telescope to restore to the treasury. You have made me realize how dependent one can become on pieces of ground glass for the expansion of one's vision.'

The Significance of the Robe

No question embarrassed the Dalai Lama when he was in touch with his holiness. When he was not, almost any question embarrassed him because he felt sure that his alienation from Godhood would be exposed in answers that came out sounding either pompous or flip.

His infrequent lapses into the pretentious or vulgar were not supposed to occur since he was assumed to be a source of perpetual enlightenment. That he suffered temporary periods of spiritual dullness was a secret even his closest tutors, if they were aware of it, would never have acknowledged to his face; but he wondered if perhaps it wasn't the subject of court gossip. When he knew that divinity was with him, he was always in a marvelous humor and consequently his answers were humorous, even comic. But when God had left him stranded, he would find himself taking on a very stern expression and speaking with appalling seriousness. The lamas of his court weren't fooled, he was sure, but most foreigners were. They were forever quoting things he had said when his God was far from him while ignoring his truly holy pronouncements which always sounded to them like some kind of joke.

Unlike some wise men – his friend Dr Klune, for example – who take one holy truth unto themselves and then tour the world repeating it over and over again, the Dalai Lama had decided to speak from now on mostly in parables, never allowing himself to tell the same story twice. As the original creative genius of Tibet, he renounced all dogmatic statements, resolving to speak from the purely intuitive inspiration of the moment. Prepared language lacking spontaneity was forsaken even though the rituals that surrounded his every activity remained extremely traditional. Part of his daily discipline was to condition his mind never to anticipate a question.

For their part, people who sought audience with the Dalai Lama were asked to put aside all carefully rehearsed questions and to let the truly honest wonderment that was hiding within them be drawn out by the king when he looked into their eyes. The supplicant must learn to abandon control of the questions, to relax until the words come out as in a dream.

One lady tourist from Australia had spent two full months in a cave trying to rid her mind of questions so that the right one would emerge *de novo* at the moment the Dalai Lama asked her to speak. Now, having presented him with ceremonial scarves, here she was seated beneath him. He looked into her eyes with a grin. He really felt at one with himself today. He knew he couldn't miss.

'Speak, Madam.'

The woman opened her mouth, expecting some profoundly mystical question to come whispering out. Instead, she found herself saying, in a kind of voice she used back home on the telephone, 'Why in the world does a monk wear a long robe instead of shirt and pants?' Blushing furiously, she tried to control herself, but her voice went right on. 'Does a monk wear anything underneath?'

She glanced around with dismay to see that the assembled monks were gasping. (It was a gasp of shock, for the gasp of amazement had been banned.) But the Dalai Lama remained quite calm and was full of sympathy for the woman's distress. He was in such a good mood that he even stood up on his cushions and did a little dance before answering.

'Our robe is like the mountains of Tibet,' he said. 'It rises from our feet to form a peak above our head. Though we come from heaven, the robe shows that we are grounded in the earth. The higher one climbs our mountains, the headier one becomes. When you feel most giddy, Madam, you are in our mind. You are on the dizzy peak where the air is most refined and visions come most easily. You gaze down upon the world as we gaze down upon our own body, which flows without interruption, as you can see, into our feet.

'There is enough space between our robe and the ground so that the air can flow freely over us, being warmed by our flesh. If we wore a shirt and pants, the flow of air would be interrupted. Even worse, we could not enjoy the unimpeded movement of our clothes over our body. We must be able to move so freely within our robe that when we turn our hands or our body to either side – like so – the robe doesn't move at all. You see? Thus does the Great Spirit move inside the mountain.'

The woman was listening with fascination now. Her eyebrows were raised so high that they disappeared into her hair. Something lascivious in her expression, however, had brought the Dalai Lama to a sudden stop. His spirit fell from the heights of its humor and he began to blush severely, glancing around at members of his cabinet for someone who might come to his rescue. Besides the old Regent, there were the Secretary of Interior Life, the Secretary of the Heart's Treasury, the Secretary of Health, Renunciation and Wisdom, the Secretary of Priestly and Prophetic Equilibrium, the Secretary of Peace, the Secretary of Birth and Rebirth, the Secretary of Savoir-Faire.

It was this last cabinet minister who rose and came to

the aid of his king. The Secretary of Savoir-Faire had been educated in Indochina by the French and was always ready to cope with situations that could only be overcome by the most delicate language.

'My dear Madam,' he began, 'if you will be so very kind as to allow me to respond for my Lord and to employ myself as a living witness to your curiosity, so that his gentle presence might not be disturbed by a subject perhaps too disturbing to his exalted station and sensibilities.'

The woman turned and was startled by the dashing smile of this dignitary. 'Certainly,' she said.

Meanwhile, the Dalai Lama had closed his eyes and was entering into a discreet trance.

'You will understand,' said the secretary in most delicate tones, 'that we monks could never practice the deceit of wearing shorts under our robes, for our people must know that we have nothing to hide. Observe my robe, for example. Quite obviously it covers my flesh, therefore it hides nothing. But to wear something under the robe to hide the special magnificence that covers it would be deception indeed. Also, every part of me must have that loose and joyous quality of a swinging bell.

'Should I be aroused by any of my people, whether spiritually, intellectually or sensually, they should know of it, for the women receive great blessing regarding the *mysterium tremendum*. On certain feast days, there are even monks among us who serve as testimonials of fertility in such wise that the women are even permitted to enter their robes – with the greatest tact and reverence, of course. There should be adequate space for the performance of those worshipful oblations that ensue. No, Madam, trousers would decidedly not do.'

The Dalai Lama had calmed himself during this rescuing discourse and was now coming out of his trance. He opened

his eyes to discover that the Australian lady was nowhere
to be seen. For an instant, he was bewildered, but a certain
expression of glee on the face of the Secretary of Savoir-
Faire assured him that she was still somewhere in the
room, modestly hidden while she expressed appropriate
thanksgiving for the fertile vision that had been granted
her.

A Bubbling Brook

'TELL me, Dr Klune,' said the Dalai Lama, 'during your travels in the United States of America, what have you heard them say about us?'

'Unfortunately,' said Klune, 'mention of Tibet is usually limited to a single rather condescending tale that never fails to provoke much laughter. I have heard the tale so often that I've begun to wonder whether it doesn't have some basis in fact. Perhaps you could enlighten me on this.'

Klune then proceeded to tell about the American who travels the world over searching without success for a man who can satisfy him with an answer to his question What is the meaning of life? While all the great philosophers profess bewilderment, they are in accord that a certain hermit living in a nearly inaccessible mountain region of Tibet does know the answer. Although no Westerner has ever been able to survive the arduous journey to this hermit's cave, the American decides to set forth. He sells all that he has, quits his job, abandons his wife and children. Five years later, after many setbacks and enormous suffering, he comes within sight of the fabled cave; and, sure enough, there at the entrance sits the hermit, his eyes sparkling merrily. The exhausted American approaches and ventures to ask, 'Is it true, O Wise One, that you know the meaning of life?'

'Why, certainly,' answers the hermit.

'Would you by any chance be willing to disclose this great secret to me?'

'Gladly.'

'Gladly?' Overwhelmed with gratitude, the American prepares to prostrate himself at the hermit's feet.

'Life,' proclaims the hermit, beaming, 'is a bubbling brook.'

The American draws back aghast. 'You mean to tell me,' he screams, 'that I've come all the way up here, that I've abandoned everything I treasured in life, that I've struggled to learn your language, that I've endured innumerable diseases, injuries, hardships beyond belief only to have you tell me that life is a bubbling brook!'

'Well,' says the hermit, chagrined, 'isn't it?'

The Dalai Lama was much amused by the story. He said that he knew the hermit quite well, having taken lessons in speech with him. 'My guess,' he told Dr Klune, 'is that the hermit was right here with me in the Potala at the time the story takes place, and that the person to whom the American spoke in his delirium was none other than a bubbling brook near the cave into which the hermit had poured his presence.'

'The hermit was your speech tutor?' asked Klune.

'No,' said the king, 'he and I were students together. It was my second year in power. I was five years old when they brought the hermit in to share my studies with me. Shortly after I was crowned, he had caused great excitement by returning to the palace after a forty-year absence. Few are the monks who leave the Potala for a life of solitary meditation; and of those who leave, the ones who return are rare indeed, for it is understood that when a monk returns it is because he is ready to preach a truth never before revealed to man.

'Rumors had been circulating for years that this hermit had discovered the secret of life itself. During all his years in the cave, he had never spoken, but the radiance of his face suggested such at-oneness with nature that none could doubt his supreme enlightenment. When he sat down in the courtyard in the place where the preaching is done, a crowd gathered at once. He said not a word but waited until the great lamas from all over Tibet had been given time to journey to Lhasa. At last, after weeks had passed and the multitude was complete, he raised his arms to ask for silence. All the monks leaned forward to listen with bated breath. The hermit opened his mouth. A strange sound came forth. The monks cocked their heads to listen more closely. Some were bewildered, others amused. All were disappointed. They could not make out any words. The most they could hear was the sound of a bubbling brook. The hermit saw the looks on their faces, blushed, and closed his mouth.

'The next day, he opened his mouth again. This time the congregation heard a rushing torrent in the spring. On other days they heard waterfalls, the riffle of shallow water over stones, the pounding of waves on an ocean shore, fast water and slow water, and sometimes water so still that nothing could be heard save the occasional splash of a fish breaking the surface. But never a word.

'Some of the younger monks had begun to snicker quite mercilessly, although they must have been able to see that the hermit was making every effort to form words and felt quite heartsick about his failure. He would shake his head each day after trying, blush furiously and slowly close off the sounds of running water that issued from his lips. Then he would lower his head in defeat and gather strength for yet another effort the next day.

'Finally, the high lamas consulted and decided that after

so many years of solitude the hermit had forgotten the Tibetan language and needed to be taught once more like a child so that he might construct his wisdom into intelligible phrases. I was just learning to speak the language of the court at that time, so it was decided the hermit should work with me under the same tutor. The old man and I became fast friends. I even helped him formulate the crude phrases that enabled him finally to address the congregation. Would you like to hear what he said before he departed once more for his cave?'

'I certainly would, Highness,' said Dr Klune. 'But let me guess. Did he say that life is a bubbling brook?'

The king smiled. 'He told us that below his cave was a brook into whose waters he had stared for forty years. He said that if we wished to hear what he had to say we would have to go talk to the brook since he himself had ceased to feel natural with human speech. "Brothers," he said, "I am not with you now. I am with the brook."

'A zealous young monk said that he wished, then, to hasten to the brook but that he had heard it was in a most inaccessible place, very hard to find. "You need not look for the brook," replied the hermit, "for the brook is here with you now. The brook is me. If you wish to stare into water, you may stare into my eyes." He proceeded to tell how he had sat down long ago to meditate by a brook. As the years passed, he became the water and was carried downstream until he grew into a river. Roots of vegetation reached out to drink him while his own roots hurried through the ground until he found himself rising up through the stems of flowers, blossoming into lakes, spreading little veins across the earth, rising toward the heavens, forming clouds and raining down. Fish were flitting through his arms. He thrust himself up one particular spire or spine to find himself bursting forth in an enormous bloom — an ocean large and golden as the sun. He was carried down into its whirling center until sucked into a fissure in the earth. Through the split rock he traveled until he came to a place where the river was born. He issued forth from a hole in the ground and became a small trickle that became a brook. The brook passed a place where he was sitting in the mouth of a cave staring into the water. He passed through his own eyes and continued to pass through himself until the brook became him and he became the brook.

'What he had to say to his brothers was this: That rivers are the bloodstream of the earth and the earth is a creature like ourselves sitting on the edge of the cosmos watching the ether stream by over the stars, watching through the eyes of men and becoming ever more a part of what it sees.'

The Trance-Walker

A FAMOUS trance-walker, the Master of Lung-gom, had started on his way to the Potala to pay his respects to the king just on the day when the bridge he would have to cross over the River Gniman was washed out by a flood. Learning of this, the Dalai Lama summoned forty of his most robust young monks and told them to hasten to the river to build a new bridge, lest the Master of Lung-gom, who was known to suffer from a defect of vanity, attempt to cross the torrent and drown; for there is an old Tibetan proverb, 'Even a man in a trance can be swallowed by his own vanity.'

The monks set to work cutting down trees in the forest near the river to make a span. Ten monks had trimmed one tree and were now carrying it on their shoulders down the steep, rocky slope to the river when the weight of the log began to propel them forward at an ever increasing speed. They found themselves rushing downward unable to stop, their heads thrown back, feet flying over the jagged rocks. A kind of giddiness overcame them as they realized how swiftly and smoothly they were skimming the ground without anyone turning his ankle or otherwise injuring his feet.

Only at the last second did the monks realize they were at the bank of the river about to fling themselves into the torrent. Simultaneously, they let out a scream, dug in their heels and sent the log hurtling ahead of them like a giant spear. It sailed beautifully through the air and settled astride the river just as they normally would have placed it through long hours of toil. Exhilarated, the monks sat on the bank giggling and hugging each other for a long time before they climbed the slope to tell their brothers.

The other monks joined the game and soon there were four teams of ten monks each, running down the slope with a log on their shoulders to hurl across the river. By the time a wide bridge had been laid, they were addicted.

When the Master of Lung-gom reached the bridge, he crossed over without really knowing whether there was a river beneath his feet. One need not have worried since he could have walked on the water just as easily. He had been walking for two days in a deep trance, his eyes so fixed by night on a certain star and by day on a certain imaginary bird in the sky that no sound or sight beneath his feet need have concerned him. His vanity was entirely subdued, his only thought being to prostrate himself before the Dalai Lama as soon as possible to receive his blessing. He had chosen the least traveled way so that few people would observe his miraculously swift passage and stop to gape. In short, he was as free of himself and as tuned in to the universe as he ever would be.

But when he came up the slope from the River Gniman, he was brought to a sudden stop by an astonishing sight. A tree trunk some hundred feet long was seen arching through the sky above the highest pines. He opened his ears to hear the echoes of a powerful scream as the missile went crashing back down into the greenery. His trance broken, he stood in the forest with legs suddenly trembling with fatigue, assailed by pangs of hunger from his long fast. He peered into the forest to see what looked like a gigantic many-legged dragon rushing at full speed through the trees. But, no, it was the trunk of another tree being carried on the shoulders of ten monks in burgundy and saffron robes. The monks came to a stop and, with an insane scream that made the pine needles shiver, sent their tree trunk hurtling up through the forest.

Thus interrupted and thrown into his weakest condition, the Master of Lung-gom met the monks who had come to build the bridge for him. How senseless it seemed to be doing the trance walk that forty novice monks could do for him with such obvious joy. Had they not achieved together in a few days what he alone had worked at for fifteen arduous years?

He instructed them to attach a platform between two of the logs they had been sporting with and thus to carry him on their shoulders to the king. Of course, the monks were delighted to do so, and it was quite a sight to see these forty brutes with their palanquin of rough-hewn logs come rushing through the streets of Lhasa and up the steps to the Potala while the serene master of walking in a trance sat up there on his platform smiling beatifically.

An envoy from Japan happened to be in Lhasa at the time. Witnessing this spectacle, he asked the Dalai Lama whether these monks and their master could be sent to give a demonstration of their powers at the cherry blossom festival in Kyoto. He said that, while the art of 'human floats' or 'platform running' was already well known in Japan, he had never seen it done at such speed and without apparent injury to the feet.

The Dalai Lama made the mistake of acquiescing. What ensued is best described by a Mr Snyder in a letter to the London *Times*.

During the cherry blossom festival in Kyoto, it has long been the custom for groups of young men representing different fraternal orders to rush through the streets chanting with enormous floats carried on their shoulders.

The Trance-Walker

A Tibetan holy man and his retinue brought new life to the festival last May when they were able to carry their float over beds of nails and burning coals without apparent suffering. I witnessed the spectacle and can report that the forty or so young monks were guided in this feat by an old man who sat on a golden cushion near the back of the float beating a drum and urging them on much as a coxswain would his crew.

Since the festival six months ago, groups of young men all over Japan have been teaming up in efforts to duplicate this feat. Many groups have collapsed on the burning coals and died writhing in agony, but the majority have survived to form élite corps of what are now called The Rams.

These same Rams can be seen rushing through the streets of Kyoto with logs on their shoulders, ten men to a log, knocking down anything that dares cross their path. Sometimes they go into fierce trances and, urged on by a leader who sits precariously perched on the log above them chanting the rhythm, take to knocking down the walls of those houses and business establishments run by their enemies. These enemies are 'bourgeois individualists' whom they consider decadent holdovers of the capitalist mentality.

The mystique of these battering-ram bullyboys requires absolute submission to the will of the group. Any person who attempts to stand out from society is attacked – his very walls knocked down. Their chant is *We*, chanted faster and faster as the destroyer-floats move through frightened crowds toward the opponent.

Hoping to redeem himself and to impress the Japanese people once more with the potential of individual discipline, the Tibetan holy man who started it all made the mistake one day of coming down from his platform and walking without assistance over a bed of coals. This exhibitionism was considered so rude to the notion that all men must work together for a common destiny, and so profanely vain – even by the holy man's own retinue of monks – that he was stoned to death without their lifting a hand to protect him.

News about the death of the Master of Lung-gom was what prompted the Dalai Lama to say to his retinue as they prepared to flee into exile, 'While we are abroad, let us not exhibit vain tricks and trances.'

The Chamber of Horrors

ONE evening, when the Dalai Lama was still a small child, his tutors came to him with great sympathy and told him as gently as they could that it was time for him to be locked into the chamber of horrors, for he had been heard crying out in his sleep.

They explained that he could not be a wise king until he had learned to overcome his fears. The ancient gods of Tibet were to be his guides into courage. These gods would appear to him in the masks of his various earthly and illusory fears, upon which he must meditate nightly until fear was cast out by the love of life.

The boy was taken down a narrow passageway to a door opening upon darkness. He was told to enter the room and sit on the floor. A very dim lamp was placed next to him. The tutors withdrew, closing the door and locking it from the outside.

At first the Dalai Lama saw nothing but a kind of altar, then hideous faces began to loom out at him. He shrieked, sprang up and threw himself at the door. When the tutors finally opened it, the limp body of the king slid out and slumped at their feet in a dead faint. They carried him to bed and sang him lullabies all night long to ease his terrible dreams.

The next night he was taken to the chamber of horrors once more. This time he sat there with eyes shut tight.

Though trembling violently, he managed to stay in his place until released.

Months passed before he dared open his eyes in the chamber of horrors again. But, once he had understood that he would no longer be allowed the quest for truth without passing through terror and that his cowardice would only condemn him to a lifetime of returns to this dreaded place, he began to peek briefly and, finally, with wide-open eyes at the horrifying personages. Every one of them seemed fiendishly bent on doing him harm.

However, after long periods of dread followed by nightmares and sleepless nights, he began to lose his fear of one mask and then another until, at last, all the masks had become his friends. When the Dalai Lama left Tibet to escape into India, he visited the chamber of horrors last of all to bid good-bye to the beautiful masks of the gods.

Here is the way he described the masks to one who was with him on this occasion:

'The one barely visible in the corner I feared most of all because it refused to make itself known. The very thought of its vague, featureless presence destroyed my sense of certainty. I was filled with uneasiness about everything on earth that persistently refuses to emerge from the darkness. It was only after my kingdom became threatened by a growing class of inspectors, analysts, spies and scientific clarifiers morbidly fascinated with unlocking and labeling the so-called secrets of Tibet that I realized my task was one of restoring the known to the unknown. As I came to understand that one is illumined by awe, I realized how the evershadowy mask was inviting me to my own destiny — that of an actor called upon to increase the tremendous mystery of holiness.

'Over there you see what in my childhood seemed the

terrifying image of my own adulthood. It showed me myself as the fool I would become, burdened with an exalted image that my naive words and ineffectual actions would increasingly belie. I saw that as I grew up my importance would grow down. Already, that other face next to the bewildered, bespectacled caricature of a Dalai Lama in exile was mocking me, mocking my struggle to become more than what history condemned me to be, deriding me as one who would become less and less in men's religious imaginations until he was nothing but a decadent old king with a silly grin sitting somewhere in exile as a kind of political curiosity, the subject of ill-informed stories and pseudo-mystical speculations.

'Then, one sunny afternoon when I was feeling very grandiose about my divine powers, I took it into my head that I could step off my palanquin and fly into the sky like a kite. Instead, I fell flat on my face in front of an enormous crowd that had come to celebrate my dignity. When I awoke the next day to learn that my social *faux pas* (so to speak) had not alienated me from the affection of my people but had increased their spiritual humors by giving them something more to be jolly about, I understood that if you are willing to make a fool of yourself God will be willing to make you wise. The mask that had mocked me became a comrade in merriment, while the mask of the fool changed into a friendly promise of old age.

'As for the mask of the relentless pursuer, I stopped wishing I could flee from him when I finally despaired of escaping. While I wished not to have my life taken from me, I wished more hysterically to be rid of the fear of having it taken, so I yielded to the onslaught. The masked terror that sprang upon me destroyed, if not my life, my attachment to this particular form of life, and thereby revealed to me my eternal self. The mask only wished to scare hell out of me, as the English say, in order to open my way to heaven.

'Gazing at my own death mask was the hardest ordeal to overcome. Only as I learned by meditation to move back through time to earliest memory did I realize that I was looking at the face of a child peacefully asleep in his mother's womb. I saw that my death was full of promise, and I ceased at last to fear for my life.'

The Wisest Oracle

THE Dalai Lama could never make up his mind whether to flee into exile. Several times he had put together a hasty caravan and departed in the night only to turn back somewhere along the way after catching sight of the people's forlorn faces when they learned he was deserting them. After it became certain that the Chinese Red Guards were already on their way to Lhasa with plans to make him a subject of ridicule and torture, he summoned the famous Oracle Priest of Kundar, of whom there was no peer.

This man could read the stars and the entrails of birds with equal ease. He could talk with animals and spirits. He could visit the past and travel into the future. He could hypnotize, teleport, levitate, do magic. But, most impressive of all, he could go into his 'whirlwind of sound and fury,' during which the guardian spirits of ancient Tibet would take possession of him and speak through his mouth.

The Oracle of Kundar arrived at the palace in a jovial mood to report that all the signs above and below the earth agreed. Now he had only to go into his whirlwind trance to receive final confirmation from the spirits.

The Dalai Lama and his monks formed a wide circle in the ceremonial hall while the Oracle sat down at the center. 'Never fear, Majesty,' he said. 'The guardians will guide you in your decision.' Without further ado, he closed his eyes and waited to be possessed. One by one, the spirits entered his body, sending one arm flying, then the other. Both legs jerked out as the Oracle went into a spastic seizure, twitching and squirming across the floor. Suddenly he sprang high into the air and began to spin like a top gone berserk. The monks drew back cautiously, for he was a huge man and the flaying of his limbs had been known to kill innocent bystanders.

As he spun again high toward the ceiling, his arms became tangled in the hanging banners which were brought down snapping and crackling around him. Candles, benches and statuary flew in all directions. Never had the Oracle attained such a frenzy. The seven-foot-tall palace guards rushed in to restrain him as he lunged dangerously close to the throne, but he knocked them all away before ripping a stone from the floor and bringing it down repeatedly on his own head as if in a desperate effort to stun himself. His face was running with blood.

Again the guards rushed him and again he tore himself away, this time smashing his fists so hard into a pillar that the walls shook and bones could be heard to snap. Shrieking with pain, he fell to the floor. The whole agony of Tibet about to be crushed by a foreign power was contained in the powerful bellows that left everyone wide-eyed and terrified except the Dalai Lama, who felt elated that the spirits had come to speak to him at last. He signaled the guards to leap upon the Oracle and hold him down so that the official interpreter could decipher the meaning of the cries.

When the great Oracle had passed out and the guards had carried him gently away, the Dalai Lama eagerly called the interpreter to his side. 'Tell me quickly what guidance I've been given.'

'Ah, Your Holiness,' the interpreter said, 'you are most

fortunate. The ancient spirits have agreed with all the other signs. They are of one accord.'

'And what do they say I should do?'

'They say you should not look to outward signs to tell you what to do.'

A few days later, the Dalai Lama departed for India with no lingering doubts whatsoever. He has stayed there to this day.

The Father's Father

THE most beautiful parts of his father's body were the feet which had danced around the room every morning to greet the sun for as long as he could remember. His father often had let the sun go down upon his anger, but he never failed to wake up rejoicing. Now, his God son knelt and removed the fur-lined slippers. The soles of the feet were as hard as the rocks he had spent most of his life scrambling over while herding his sheep, but the upper surfaces were of a delicate, pale color, smooth and soft as silk and speckled with brown sun splotches.

The Dalai Lama kissed his father's warm feet. Death had not reached them yet. It had come first to his heart and then to his chest. Nor was his mind gone. Though the eyes were rolled up with all light extinguished, the dead man seemed to be listening intently not only through his ears but through his nostrils and mouth while the lama, who was to guide him through the confusion of the spirit world into the realm of light from whence he could survey his choices for a new incarnation, calmly explained the dangers he would have to face along the way and gave instructions on how to overcome them.

Leaning back, still holding one of his father's feet, the Dalai Lama went into his father's mind to ask, 'Did you ever know how much I loved you?' But this was no longer the dead man's concern. The Dalai Lama wept, not for sorrow but for the fragile beauty of this man who even now was sending the peculiar merriment of the morning sun down through the foot and into his son's hand. A streak of fire shot up the Dalai Lama's arm as his father gave a last push and leaped into the cosmos.

The old man had died well, without violent protest or unseemly noise. Though it was not the magnificent death of a high lama, who can leave his body so quietly that sometimes he will have been sitting in a lotus position, dead for several days, before his departure is discovered, still this death was sweet and modest enough in the way it kept its secret to leave the king deeply moved.

The Dalai Lama had arrived at his father's mansion just in time to see the old man smile quietly, cock his head as if listening to a birdsong, and then slump forward with only a faint gurgling in his throat. As with every son with a destiny of his own, something inside the boy cried out with relief at a kind of love that has been spent at last; and with agony at taking on a new, more powerful emotion of mature filial love.

No longer the invention of his father, the Dalai Lama knew he was free now to invent himself. The lama handed him a sealed letter that his father had written for him just the day before. He went outside to sit in the garden and read it.

Every one of us, my son, populates the world with his imagination. The greatest of us creates a religious system and becomes both its sinner and its saint. So was it with the Buddha, so was it with Jesus, and so can it be with you if you'll start loving yourself, which, I promise you, will come more easily now that you can stop hating me.

Stung to the quick, the Dalai Lama wanted to rush back into the house and tell his father that he had never hated him. He had only resented him for always leaving the question Am I nothing more than the extension of your imagination? unanswered. But why trouble a dead man? The Dalai Lama stayed where he was on the bench under the trees and let his memory flash back to the night of his second birthday.

His father had carried him downstairs to where the cattle slept, there to talk about the great project they were to share all their lives as a blood secret never to be revealed to anyone.

The secret was this: That, poor as they were, his mother and father soon would be living in a luxurious home in Lhasa with many gardens and servants, all the food and drink they desired and no need ever to work again. 'And you,' the father had whispered, 'you, my brilliant little spawn, are going to give all this to me by becoming a person even more splendid than I shall be. You are going to become the Dalai Lama.'

'Dada,' was all the infant could say. 'Lala.'

'All you need is a little practice. Practice makes perfect and perfect makes God. You may hurt under the arms for a while, but it won't last long and once you're God you'll have an eternity of painless bliss, from incarnation to incarnation, until we all live in the kingdom of heaven.

'In less than two years,' his father had said, 'you'll be taken in glory to the great city of Lhasa, there to be crowned while all the people buzz around you like bees around a queen. Tomorrow I send your brother to the monastery where I expect him to become a great theologian, a chronicler of God, but you will be the God Himself.'

Every night after that, he would join his father in their secret meeting place to undergo the wounding of his sides and the pulling of his ears so that he might come to resemble the long-eared Buddha manifested in the four-armed Chenrezi, sire of the Tibetan people, incarnated in the Dalai Lamas. The wounds on his trunk eventually left the necessary scars. But mere physical signs would not suffice to impress those wise men who would come one day disguised as poor shepherds searching for the new incarnation.

When the lamas and monks finally cast off their disguises, he must be able to recognize the monasteries from whence they came. This could be learned, since each of the monasteries had its peculiar style and color of robe. But far more difficult would be the final test of his confirmation when certain bells, rosaries, toys and trinkets belonging to the thirteenth Dalai Lama were handed to him to identify from amongst many other objects. For this he would have to depend on various subtle clues: the eagerness of the lama who handed him the objects, the peculiar character traits of the thirteenth Dalai Lama – his fascination with mechanical gadgets, his love of sports cars (therefore, toy cars), his tendency to keep things neat and polished, etc.

There was the problem of making the house appear just like the red one with the white roof which people in the marketplace said the Gachung Oracle had seen in a vision. Yes, a great deal of work had to be done before the task was accomplished, and his father was still putting the final touches of red paint on the wall when the wise men arrived to find the child playing in the kitchen.

The Dalai Lama wasn't the least bit nervous as he called the lamas by the names of their monasteries without even seeing the robes hidden under their shepherd's cloaks. He had no trouble at all identifying the correct objects. When he saw the bell and the rosary and the toy Rolls-Royce, he seized them as if they truly belonged to him. The lamas were as familiar as his father. In fact, his father seemed suddenly strange with those awkward pretenses of surprise.

Only a few years after his coronation, the Dalai Lama had so thoroughly removed those first years from his mind that he would ask himself quite naively, Why do I tug at my ears in secret? And when he stood before the mirror with upraised arms looking at the scars left by his Chenrezi arms, he only wondered what it must have felt like when he could hold a candle in one hand, a bowl in another, a stone in the third and a bird in the fourth.

The only time that it would all come back to him was on one of his father's infrequent visits to the Potala. These visits filled him with sudden turmoil. He was forever sending messages to his father and mother to come see him, yet when the old man was actually there he was very soon wishing to see him gone.

The Dalai Lama, seated on a platform above his father, would look down at the slightly mischievous eyes and wonder: Am I truly a creation of my own or am I the mere creation of my father? Can it be that my father, whom I have flattered myself into regarding as less spiritually developed than myself, is the true Dalai Lama who only uses me as a fulfillment and manifestation of his covert God-Self? Is my father, this *bon vivant* gambler, entertainer and lover of women, the material ground in which my spiritual life is rooted or am I fed from my own source?

'Father,' he would ask, 'who dwells in me? If you dwell in me, who dwells in you? Are we nothing but echoes of some original name that was cried out long ago against the great mountains and is heard returning ever more dimly across the valleys? Is the world truly running down? Am I less than you?'

His father's eyes would fill with sly hints, but the answer was never more than a grin that seemed to apologize for his having abandoned his son to the rigors of palace life while he himself sported with abandon down below.

The Dalai Lama would have liked his father just once to confess their complicity, but he could not bring himself to drop more than vague hints – as when he said how fondly he remembered those nights when the two of them had sat among the cattle planning the future.

To such remarks, the old man would shrug. 'I'm a senile old fool with a poor memory.'

'Do you remember when the lamas came to choose me as their king?'

'What I remember or don't remember matters little, Your Eloquence.'

'It matters a great deal to me.'

'All that matters is that people had a choice. They could believe in a world that has meaning and order thanks to the ongoing providence of a god, or they could believe the world is a madhouse. Belief is self-fulfilling. They made the right choice.'

'Tell me then why you came to see me when you knew we could never speak frankly to each other again. Perhaps you found it hard to believe that God was nothing more than the creation of your own ambition.'

'So He is for all of us. Our ambition is to be men, therefore we create gods.'

At the end of their last visit, a sudden wave of resentment had swept over the king. 'Or is it that you're hungry for some credit, Father. You don't dare take credit in the town so you come up here to get credit from me.' Already his father had disappeared down a hallway, but the Dalai Lama leaped from his throne and pursued him. 'You're *not* God, you know. *I* am.'

Way down the hallway, his father turned. The Dalai Lama stopped and studied that smug grin so clearly visible by the light of numerous butter lamps. It seemed to say, Good for you. Or was it saying, Good for me. But, no, it was saying with self-satisfaction, Good for all of us. That would not do.

Enraged, the Dalai Lama started to scream, but before the words were out, his father had signaled with a finger across his lips. It was the old familiar gesture given after those lessons on the farm before they both went back up to bed, and the Dalai Lama's words now refused to come out in more than a whisper. 'You did not create me. I used your schemes to create myself. We were all on to your tricks. We just used them as a bridge to the heavenly fields.'

But his father hadn't heard. Running on tiptoe, the Dalai Lama caught up with him, grabbed him and wheeled him around. 'Father. You're old and you may die and I may never know for sure. Did you really ever prepare me for all this or was I dreaming?'

The old man seemed visibly to shrink. His milky eyes blinked confusedly. 'Who *is* your father?' he muttered. 'Don't you know by now that he's dreaming us both? He's dreaming you as a god and me as a man, so be a god and let me be a man.' Removing the boy's hand from his shoulder, he hobbled away.

Once more the Dalai Lama had returned to his private chapel to sit beneath the images carved in gold.

Now, as he sat in the garden, he looked at the small wooden bridge arching over a pond and remembered that the battle was over. His father had crossed to the heavenly fields. The phrase came to him that has come to so many other sons when they make peace at last with their creator: I am that I am.

MORE ABOUT PENGUINS
AND PELICANS

Penguinews, which appears every month, contains details of all the new books issued by Penguins as they are published. From time to time it is supplemented by our stocklist, which includes around 5,000 titles.

A specimen copy of *Penguinews* will be sent to you free on request. Please write to Dept EP, Penguin Books Ltd, Harmondsworth, Middlesex, for your copy.

In the U.S.A.: For a complete list of books available from Penguins in the United States write to Dept CS, Penguin Books, 625 Madison Avenue, New York, New York 10022.

In Canada: For a complete list of books available from Penguins in Canada write to Penguin Books Canada Ltd, 2801 John Street, Markham, Ontario L3R 1B4.

DAVID STOREY

THIS SPORTING LIFE

This is an exceptional first novel in these days, because the characters are concerned with expressing themselves in physical, not emotional or intellectual, terms.

The world in which the story is set is that of professional Rugby League football in an industrial northern city. It covers several years in the life of the narrator, Arthur Machin, from the day of his inclusion in the local team to the match when he begins to feel age creeping up on him and his feet failing. David Storey recounts the fortunes of his gladiator hero with little sentimentality and with all the harsh reality of grime, mud, sweat, intrigue, and naked ambition.

FLIGHT INTO CAMDEN

Acclaimed as a remarkable young writer for his first novel, *This Sporting Life*, David Storey was awarded the 1961 John Llewellyn Rhys Memorial Prize for *Flight into Camden*.

This moving story is recounted by Margaret, the daughter of a Yorkshire miner, who falls in love with a married teacher and goes to live with him in a room in Camden Town, London.

'A love story written with seriousness, sensibility, and intensity' – *Observer*

and

PASMORE

RADCLIFFE

A TEMPORARY LIFE

THE MIDAS CONSEQUENCE

Michael Ayrton

In a restaurant in the south of France, an old Italian sculptor holds court. He has climbed to the pinnacle of his art, received the bounty of the gods; all he touches turns to gold.

'There are flickers of thunder and bursts of lightning, and real myth horror ... this is one of the few novels about an artist which rings true, and rings with a drama which will still clang in the reader's mind long after he has finished' – *Books and Bookmen*

NO PLACE LIKE: SELECTED STORIES

Nadine Gordimer

'A magnificent collection worthy of all homage' – Graham Greene in the *Observer* Books of the Year 1976

With this collection of thirty-one stories Nadine Gordimer displays all her descriptive power and acute insight, pinning Africa to the page like a butterfly for our inspection.

'This dazzlingly rich, impressively solid selection ... The scrupulous intensity of her regard shouts from the opening sentences' – Valentine Cunningham in the *New Statesman*

FOREIGN AFFAIRS

Sean O'Faolain

'The finest collection of stories to come out of Ireland for many years' – *Hibernia*

Eight stories from the acknowledged master of Irish letters. They deal in love and strangeness, from Dublin to Brussels to the crumbled remains of ancient Sybaris, delineating with wit and colour the silent spaces between lovers.